JOY
BEYOND
GRIEF

*A new understanding of grief
with gentle and practical exercises
to help you.*

Janice Thompson

BALBOA.PRESS
A DIVISION OF HAY HOUSE

Balboa Press books may be ordered through booksellers or by contacting:

Balboa Press
A Division of Hay House
1663 Liberty Drive
Bloomington, IN 47403
www.balboapress.com
844-682-1282

Because of the dynamic nature of the Internet, any web addresses or links contained in this book may have changed since publication and may no longer be valid. The views expressed in this work are solely those of the author and do not necessarily reflect the views of the publisher, and the publisher hereby disclaims any responsibility for them.

The author of this book does not dispense medical advice or prescribe the use of any technique as a form of treatment for physical, emotional, or medical problems without the advice of a physician, either directly or indirectly. The intent of the author is only to offer information of a general nature to help you in your quest for emotional and spiritual well-being. In the event you use any of the information in this book for yourself, which is your constitutional right, the author and the publisher assume no responsibility for your actions.

Interior Image Credit: Carole Chevalier

Print information available on the last page.

ISBN: 979-8-7652-3716-8 (sc)
ISBN: 979-8-7652-3718-2 (hc)
ISBN: 979-8-7652-3717-5 (e)

Library of Congress Control Number: 2022922401

Balboa Press rev. date: 03/10/2023

ACKNOWLEDGEMENTS

Firstly, I would like to thank my partner Ian. He was a source of constant support and encouragement throughout the writing of this book.

I offer my gratitude to Karl Dawson, the developer of Matrix Reimprinting, and Richard Flook, the creator of Advanced Clearing Energetics – two true mentors and visionaries. If it hadn't been for their help during my own grief and subsequent training from them in their distinct techniques, this book would not even exist. And neither might I, come to that.

I would very much like to give a huge thanks to my editor Lois Rose for her professionalism during the creation of this book. Her patience and kindness towards my work was amazing and her heart-lifting communications were inspiring. And I would also like to offer my full appreciation to Carole Chevalier for the wonderful illustrations throughout this book.

I offer heartfelt thanks to the many fellow therapists that I have worked with over the years; they are far too many to mention here, but their knowledge, kindness, and collaborations have proved invaluable to me personally and professionally. Specific thanks go: To Erika Brodnock whose kind heart, wisdom, and beautiful persistence enabled me to finish this book; To Penny Croal, an extremely talented trainer and good friend, for her passion and promotion of my work and always believing in me; To Wendy Lyford, a supportive friend and source of regular encouragement. And finally, to Carol and Nick Cumber for accepting me with open arms into their community and for their pure loveliness.

FOREWORD

I first met Janice when she attended one of my training courses back in 2007. Within a short space of time I was working with her as she was crying and trying to explain what the problem was. She was extremely upset as she explained her situation. That was some fifteen years ago now and I have followed her on her journey as a friend and mentor from the pain of bereavement to the joyful place she is now with a wonderful partner, two healthy, happy daughters and a successful business.

Janice's story is explained in this book. Speaking from the heart, she openly discusses her own bereavements and her journey to get help and heal herself. However, it is not just a reflection of one person's journey; rather it is a book full of passion about helping those in pain. After several years of research, training, and working with many bereaved clients, she now wishes to share her knowledge and experience with as many people as possible.

As an EFT Master and the creator of Matrix Reimprinting, I travel extensively around the world teaching and running trainings. I meet countless people who are looking for new ways to help themselves with physical and emotional problems. Janice's specialism of working with loss has enabled her to help hundreds of people with both the psychological and physical issues associated with grief.

What Janice has done in *Joy Beyond Grief* is to help us to take a new look at loss – a twenty-first century look at grief. Janice has created a step-by-step new and innovative approach to helping anyone who has lost a loved one. She explains how the mind and body deal with grief and what you can do about it. The book is full of practical tools to help you help yourself, including Matrix Reimprinting – a remarkable tool for transforming loss.

Death and loss have become almost taboo subjects in the Western world, leaving many bereaved individuals with nowhere to turn. In helping to change this, it has been my privilege to invite Janice to be one of the speakers at my supervision days on several occasions. She has since gone on to speak at many conferences and gatherings with the aim of bringing this subject into the light and helping grievers with their pain.

What Janice has captured within the pages of this book is a gentle space for grievers to gain support and advice. This book offers hope and shows you how you can help yourself through loss. If you are recently bereaved or have been struggling for years over the loss of a loved one, I recommend you read this book and follow the advice given to help you find your way to a more peaceful, joyful life. This book is a journey from cover to cover.

Karl Dawson
Author of:
Matrix Reimprinting using EFT (co-author Sasha Allenby)
Transform Your Beliefs, Transform Your Life (co-author Kate Marillat)

DEDICATION

This book is dedicated

To my brother Trevor, and my daughters Francesca and Jasmin, with whom I have shared the pain of loss,

To all those beautiful souls no longer with us in physical form,

and

To you the reader, who has experienced loss and are open enough and brave enough to seek a new way to do grief.

CONTENTS

INTRODUCTION

'People who have been in the place of sadness
where you are now, will be there for you.'
Susan Squellati Florence

In the darkest days of grief, it can feel like you will never ever get over your loss, let alone have a life again. Your heart is aching so much. The pain is so immense, and you can't focus on anything. You probably do not believe that your emotional hell could ever be transformed into a life full of new meaning, love, and depth. I certainly didn't. My journey may reflect similarities to yours; it was tough, painful, and at some points meaningless. After the initial shock, I tried so many ways to help myself, but I seemed to go off on many unhelpful tangents. Finally, I found a way through that changed everything. A gentle, comforting, empowering way through and that is what this book is all about.

My aim is to help you so you won't have to experience any of those unhelpful tangents, which only hindered my grieving process. If you are experiencing your own dark days, feelings of being in a dense fog, numbness, deep sorrow, heartache or any other way the emotional hell of loss is expressing itself, then this is the book for you. It is a hand for you to hold, a guiding light through the seemingly unbearable days and a companion through your own unique grief. I am one of those people mentioned in the quote above, but having experienced my own sadness of loss I am now in a position to be there for you in the form of this book.

May I welcome you to *Joy Beyond Grief*. I wish I could be introducing myself to you under better circumstances than the loss of a loved one.

Firstly, I would like to offer my deepest and most sincere condolences. I would also like to reach out and offer some help for as long as you need during this time of excruciating pain. The pain of loss is immeasurable and although everybody's pain is different, I can walk with you along your own path, offering guidance to a place of peace. Dare I say at this point in the book that – yes, I will – I shall take you beyond peace to a place of joyful transformation. I understand that may seem impossible for you to comprehend at this moment in time, particularly if you are grief-stricken and your loss is very raw, but please let me assure you there is a light at the end of your dark tunnel. I know, because I'm in that light now and even if you can't even see a tiny glimmer at this moment in time, it is there. Together we shall take one small step at a time towards it.

Why I wrote this book

I decided to write this book for several reasons, but mainly because I have a deep passion to help those who are suffering and struggling with the debilitating effects of grief. Why the deep passion? Because of my own experience of loss, the pain, and the experiences that followed. I feel the help for those affected by a loss is seriously lacking – not many people know how to help those grieving. Family and friends often don't know what to say or do, and professionals such as doctors and counsellors who are well intended often do not have enough time or meaningful resources to truly help those who are grieving. I hope this book goes some way to address that. Having been on the receiving end of 'not so helpful help', I found several tools, and used a few of my own, which went a long way to lift me out of my grief. Not only did my pain subside but gradually my life was transformed. I have seen how my simple yet effective tools and techniques have helped not only myself but hundreds, if not thousands, of grieving clients I have worked with.

Who is this book for?

I have written this book for you if you have recently lost a loved one and your pain is still very raw. It is also for you if some time has passed and you are still struggling to cope with your loss. If it has been many years since your loss but things are still painful, or you are experiencing any physical issues since your loss, then please keep reading. This book is also for you if you feel you are over a loss, but things still don't feel right on some level.

If you have lost your partner, mother, father, sister, brother, or you may have lost your child, your grandparent, your aunt, your uncle ... this book is for you. It might be your niece or nephew, it might be your best friend, a work colleague, a neighbour ... whomever you have lost, I offer help to you in the pages of this book. Whether your loss took the form of a terminal illness or whether your loss came suddenly without warning, this book offers guidance and comfort from my heart to yours.

Journeying through this book

I have divided this book into three sections, each with a slightly different purpose. The first four chapters are about immediate help and awareness of where you are. The second section is very much an action-based section and includes tools to help with your pain, and the third section incorporates the bigger picture of the transformative nature of loss. At the end of each chapter there are self-love exercises to help you with various aspects of your loss. I recommend you purchase a journal, where you can write your thoughts and feelings and record your answers to questions asked throughout the book. Alternatively, there are some pages at the end of this book specifically for journaling.

Historically, we have dealt with grief by trying to ignore it, pushing it away with what I would call the Keep Yourself Busy Brigade leading the march. This approach can have serious consequences during grief. It is almost impossible to shift or experience any movement in your loss if you don't fully understand and accept where you are. So, the first four chapters guide you in identifying supportive ways to gain help from others and help yourself. With awareness comes empowerment and the ability to ease your pain.

The second part of the book is all about taking action to help yourself from what you have identified in section 1. Here you will find the practical tools I used myself and have subsequently used with hundreds of my clients. Tools that are simple, gentle, and effective, but little is known about them in mainstream grief help. This section is all about inviting you to experience some techniques which may be very new to you and may feel odd, but please remember these are techniques in which I have personally seen many people's lives changed for the better – not only in terms of easing the pain and finding a place of peace, but in transformative ways they wouldn't have even believed could be possible.

The third section has been written to show you that "just getting over your loss" or "learning to cope" are, along with the Keep Yourself Busy Brigade, concepts we have been taught and for some have now become a belief. But these concepts are not truths and if my clients are anything to go by, they are redundant comments. The enormous amount of energy produced during loss is palpable, as I am sure you are aware, but are you also aware that it can be transformed? Transformed into helping you make some sense of your loss and produce positive shifts in your life, which become a way of honouring your lost love?

Ways to use this book

I wrote this book to be a companion for you to use for however long you need it. I invite you to work through each chapter at your own pace, which means it may be months or it may be a lot longer. Your own grieving process is something unique to you and it is essential you honour that. So, do not be in a rush to finish the book; be kind and gentle with yourself and read it at a pace that feels right for you. You may read one chapter and spend some time reflecting, acting upon the advice or practising the self-love exercises before moving on – and that is perfect for you. The book is the equivalent of the tortoise, not the hare; it is not a book to race to the end of as fast as you can. That approach will not be beneficial to you. It is no quick fix, as the immense pain of loss will not go away overnight, but by following the guidance in this book, I aim to tool you up and maybe introduce you to some new ways of understanding loss – your loss. All I ask is that you stay open to the fact that beyond the pain, peace can be found and transformation can follow on from that peace. If that can happen for me and so many of my clients, it can happen for you too. So, as I hold your hand, I invite you to chapter 1.

Chapter 1

EMOTIONAL SUPPORT

'There are realities we all share, regardless of our
nationality, language, or individual tastes. As we need
food, so do we need **emotional** nourishment: love,
kindness, appreciation, and support from others.'
J. Donald Walters

ON 7ᵀᴴ JULY 1981, THE entry in my diary read: 'The worst day of my life'.
I was fourteen years old, and I had been journaling my daily activities
and feelings every night for several years. However, this entry was much
different than all that had been written before. My kind, caring, fun-loving
dad had just died after a lengthy struggle with lung cancer. The shock, the
pain, and the sadness were all acutely excruciating, but the long, dark days
after his death were equally unbearable.

My mother was hurting so much that she couldn't really help me, and my
older brother was struggling, too. A couple of extended family members
did try to help in their own way, but no one really knew what to do, and
to me, it felt like I had no support at all, apart from the kindness offered
by my wonderful best friend, who was going through her own issues, as
her parents had just divorced. She was an enormous source of support,
friendship, and love. She remains a close friend to this day.

I felt so alone, and the lack of support only amplified that loneliness.
School was generally quite a hostile place for me at that time. Mrs Cox,
my Maths teacher, and Mrs Burnette, my French teacher, showed me

compassion and empathy. I often wonder if they ever realised the massive impact that they each had on my life. I thank those two ladies from the bottom of my heart.

As time wore on, I felt increasingly alone. Up until that point, I had been an easy-going teenager, but after my father's death I became rude, aggressive, and generally disruptive. Yet with the exception of the teachers mentioned above, no other teacher or adult made a connection between the change in my behaviour and the bereavement I experienced.

My aim is not to blame anyone. It was no one's fault. I do not blame my mother, who was definitely doing the best she could. I could never blame my brother, because he was going through his own pain, and still managed to be there for me. I do not blame my extended family or teachers for their lack of understanding. I simply want to give an example of how, in such difficult times, being able to speak openly about loss is crucial.

Not having significant emotional support when I lost my father certainly had an impact on how I dealt with my loss. Which in turn had an impact on the years following his death. Ultimately, I feel that lack of emotional support was a contributing factor to my grief coming back to haunt me some twenty years later.

'People start to heal the moment they feel heard.'
Cheryl Richardson

What actually is emotional support?

Emotional support helps us to cope when our feelings are turned upside down following loss. This chapter comes at the beginning of the book for two very specific reasons:

1. Having an emotional support network will help you to deal with the pain and with all other aspects of your loss, whether it's related to finances, child support, work, the general running of your house, or whatever else you have to take care of. Just about

everything becomes easier to deal with when you have people around you helping you to cope.

2. The health of your whole body will be positively affected by the emotional support you receive. Both physical and mental wellbeing can be affected by loss, and emotional support has been shown to help in each of these areas.

    While most would agree that emotional support is a good thing, what actually constitutes 'emotional support' is harder to define.

Below are some forms it may take:

1. It can be a friend listening to you talk about your sadness.
2. It can be a relation sitting quietly with you while you cry.
3. It can be a neighbour holding your hand while you express how you feel.
4. It can be someone in the community bringing a meal to you, and then staying a while to chat.
5. It can be someone offering to accompany you on a trip outside of the house.
6. It can be a work colleague going for a walk with you.

Perhaps the most helpful piece of advice is that if the support you are getting *feels* right, that means it probably is the right support for you. As you will discover as you move through your grieving experience, with me holding your hand via this book, it's all about *feeling* your way. So, if someone is making you *feel* uncomfortable, they are more than likely not the best source of emotional support for you. It's your natural instinct and your heart's voice that you are trying to tune into, as opposed to what you have been taught to think you should do. It's *listening to your heart's intuition* that will help you choose support wisely. It's also the very thing that is hardest to do when your heart is hurting so much, but rest assured that we will address this throughout the book.

If you are not sure what I mean yet, don't worry, as all will soon become clear. In the meantime, if you feel relaxed and comfortable with someone, that will generally be positive support. And, if you don't feel comfortable, try and find someone else who does make you feel this way. Here are some pointers to finding helpful, positive support:

1. Are you able to talk openly with that person?
2. Do you *feel* their help is positive?
3. Do you *feel* comfortable in their presence?
4. Do you *feel* that they listen to what you are saying?
5. Do they sit quietly and let you express your emotions?
6. Do they offer sincere, kind words of support?

Emotional support is not:

- Being dictated to.
- Being given unwanted advice.
- Being treated as if your intellect has suddenly disappeared.

Look for gentleness, kindness, empathy, and loving words and actions from those around you. The person you look to for support doesn't have to be an expert in loss – just a beautiful soul who is willing to travel this journey with you. They don't have to always know what to do or say in response to your feelings about your loss, as long as their intention is to extend support from their heart to yours. That is a fine starting place. They will grow as a support giver by working through this book with you, and may even find that they benefit from it themselves if they have experienced loss in the past. Your grieving journey will be well supported. You could even promote them to grief buddy!

Grief buddies

A grief buddy is someone who is willing to walk alongside you during your pain journey, holding your hand both literally and figuratively. It's someone who is willing to read this book with you, to help you complete the exercises and self-help tools, and to generally get involved. Anyone who helps you through each of the exercises in the book will gain an invaluable understanding of bereavement. To have someone you can call a grief buddy is a solid form of support that can really be a major factor in helping you to move through your grieving experience in a healthy, gentle, and positive way.

> 'The friend who can be silent with us in a moment of
> despair or confusion, who can stay with us in an hour of
> grief and bereavement, who can tolerate not knowing,
> not healing, not curing ... that is a friend who cares.'
> Henri Nouwen

Do you do emotions?

'Emotional support?' I may hear you cry, 'I don't do emotions.'

If, like many people, you don't feel as though you are in touch with your emotions, or you have always tried to suppress them – perhaps feeling overwhelmed, numb or in too much pain to really understand what you are experiencing – you are certainly reading the right book. Equally, if you are someone who is in touch with how you are feeling, and you are sensitive to the full array of grief-stricken feelings (which, at this moment, I appreciate can feel like they are having a very powerful hold over you) then you too, my friend, are reading the right book.

Whether you are aware of exactly how vital a role your emotions play in your life or not, you will have a far greater understanding by the end of this book. You will have to trust me on this, but by fully experiencing, understanding, and exerting some control over your emotions, you will be better able to cope with your loss and avoid ongoing suffering. This will be a huge advantage to you in the future. So, come on, let's *do* emotions.

I invite you to consider the possibility that emotions and feelings are an integral part of us, and that, this being so, support during a highly emotional time of loss makes a lot of sense. Let's explore this a little more.

Why emotional support is so important

As humans, there are some things that are absolutely fundamental to our survival. We all know that we need water to live, and we also need food and shelter, but do you realise just how important emotional nourishment is to your wellbeing? Do you realise just how vital it is to have support and kindness from others? If you don't, you are not alone, as this is an aspect of our wellbeing that is commonly overlooked. Unfortunately, this is very much to our detriment. Bereavement can certainly highlight our need for human companionship through the feelings of loneliness and isolation that it creates. This pain can be compounded if the very person you would normally turn to for comfort in your hour of need is the same person you have lost. Seeking emotional support from those who care about you is paramount.

A study cited in Dr David Hamilton's book *Why Kindness Is Good For You*, provides evidence, in the form of MRI studies of the human brain, that when someone is seeing another person suffer, the brain area which it activates demonstrates empathy with the other person's pain. We are hardwired to care about each other. He goes on to explain the role of oxytocin (the happy hormone) in compassion and kindness. Oxytocin is a neuropeptide which is produced in both the brain and the heart, and when it enters the bloodstream, it reduces blood pressure, softens arteries, and helps create new blood vessels along with many more physiological benefits. So when you see someone hug another person for example, or when you yourself accept another's kindness at this difficult time, you feel better, and you help keep your physical body healthy, too.

David expresses this beautifully, postulating that, 'When you hug someone, oxytocin flows through both of you.'[1] (See diagram below.)

OXYTOCIN FLOWING BETWEEN TWO PEOPLE

What a wonderful example of how we are all connected and are hardwired to be kind to one another. Allow someone to hug you, accept their kindness, and you will feel better. Loss can make you feel so disconnected, and a hug can go a long way to helping you regain some emotional control. Please remember to hug them back, and allow that oxytocin to flow with all its benefits. Now, go get a hug.

Simply *talking* is another form of emotional support, and a means of feeling connected. In Pennebaker, Emmanuelle, and Bernard's 2001 paper *Disclosing and Sharing Emotion: Psychological, Social and Health Consequences*, they cite several examples of how talking about the death of a loved one can have a positive effect on one's health.[2] They include one of their own studies, in which individuals who have been able to talk about the deaths of their spouses were found to be healthier in the year following the loss. If it feels right for you to talk, then talk. If you're not quite there yet, that's OK, too.

A theme that I will reiterate throughout this book is honouring what feels right for <u>you</u>. We all experience grief differently, and therefore help will come in different forms.

Even famous people who we associate with having quite regimented views on life believed in the importance of helping one another and staying connected. Charles Darwin, regarded as the father of the Theory of Evolution, was himself a father of ten children, three of whom died. It is said that he never got over the death of his first daughter, Anne Elizabeth, and that because of this tragedy, suffering and compassion became a personal and professional area of interest for him. In his book *The Descent of Man*, he wrote, 'Sympathy is the strongest instinct of man. ... In the long history of humankind (and that of animals, too), those who learnt to collaborate and improvise most effectively have prevailed.'[3] So, even someone historically associated with the term 'survival of the fittest' could clearly see the prominent roles that sympathy and compassion play in our lives. I would go further still, and suggest that each of these is absolutely crucial during difficult times in our lives, such as when facing loss and grief. We are social, emotional animals, and we all need social and emotional support.

Having established *why* emotional support is good for you, please allow the kindness of a fellow human being to comfort and support you. It is our natural way of being.

Emotional support for children

Obviously, emotional support is vital for any child experiencing loss. If you are a parent who has lost a spouse, or you are in any way involved with a grieving child, this section may be helpful.

I have been asked on many occasions what is the best way to help children. Let me say this from the start: children are far more resilient than we give them credit for, and they are also better equipped to cope than we believe them to be – as long as they're given the right support. In my experience, for children of all ages the most helpful thing to do is just answer the questions they ask you, as and when they ask them. Be honest, straightforward, and age-specific. You don't need to tell them everything, but at the same time, do not avoid talking to them about whatever they want to know. This approach tends to be a natural and holistic way for both you and your children. It eliminates the worries about what you should or should not say, and avoids you thrusting your own aspects of loss upon them.

On occasion, you may feel that honesty is not the best approach to a question, and here it becomes crucial that you listen to your heart and gut feeling, or even discuss any uncertainties you have with someone you trust. I know that if you speak from your heart, from a loving stance, you will inevitably answer in the best way for your children at that moment in time.

Additionally, be on the lookout for when they look like they need help but are not expressing it in an obvious way. This could be when they are outwardly displaying their emotions, particularly anger or guilt. Underneath whatever emotion they are displaying, there will invariably be hurt and pain. When they are hurting, give them love and cuddles by the bucketload, and remember what David Hamilton said: 'When you hug someone, oxytocin flows through both of you.' (Oxytocin has also been shown to play a role in growth, which means that hugging is good for a child's physical development, as well as emotional reinforcement.) Loss can produce fear in all of us, and children are particularly vulnerable and may become very frightened. Be vigilant, and watch for any sign that they need some extra love and reassurance.

Some researchers have shown that, as with adults, children can suffer from physical symptoms. When children as young as two to four years old don't talk about major stressors such as loss, they have higher cortisol and autonomic nervous system levels (stress indicators), and are more prone to allergies, colds, and ear infections. My advice is to talk when they want to talk, give plenty of hugs, and provide constant reassurance that they are loved.

Also, do not be afraid to show <u>your</u> feelings. Don't try and hide what you are going through. What message do you think you are sending to a child by masking your emotions? Well, it will be something along the lines of 'You shouldn't show how you feel.' 'It isn't right how you are feeling,' or even worse, 'There is something wrong with you.' It is natural and normal to cry together while talking about the one you have lost, but you should reminisce about all of the wonderful times you experienced together, too. It is perfectly fine to cry in front of your children but remember to let them know you are there for them and they are safe with you. This will reinforce the idea that it's OK to express emotions as well as reassure them you are able to look after them even if you are upset. In the introduction, I spoke about the Keep Yourself Busy Brigade. Another one is the Stiff Upper Lip Club, and yet another one to watch out for is the Be Strong for the Children Brigade. No – be real for the children. They can totally pick up on when you're down. You can't fool them, and it will only lead to confusion. In the self-love exercises at the end of each chapter, I have specified whether the exercises are suitable for children or not, so you will find some supportive exercises throughout. There are some additional recommendations in the *Resources* section at the end of the book.

Why support isn't always sought

For many in the West, the significance of this support has gradually been eroded over the years, to the point where people now believe that they must be strong on their own, and must not, or cannot, ask for help. I believe this to be a huge mistake. We all need support at times in our lives, particularly when bereaved. We are generally given a couple of weeks off work, 'to get over it', which is absolutely ridiculous.

To hear Prince Harry speak about the loss of his mother, and how he is only now seeking help after so many years, is tragic. Prince William commented on this whole stiff upper lip attitude as not being in any way helpful, particularly when dealing with bereavement. Unfortunately, I have seen many clients who have adopted this attitude, only for their loss to come back to haunt them months or years later. This is not how it is everywhere, though. There are huge differences in how other cultures deal with loss that we could learn from. In fact, that could be a whole book in and of itself.

To give you a glimpse into how other cultures deal with death, here is an example. Now, this may sound ghoulish, but it is intended solely to highlight the differences. Some ethnic groups in Madagascar have a whole lifestyle built around death, with deceased family members being exhumed every five or seven years to be sprayed with wine and wrapped in fresh cloth. Now, I know that sounds absolutely crazy to us in the West, but how do you think they would view our 'couple of weeks and get over it' approach?

When seeking emotional support is difficult

The following are some examples of common phrases I have heard many times when working with clients.

- 'I can't ask anyone for help.'
- 'I don't like to put on people.'

- 'No one can help me. They don't know what I am going through.'
- 'So-and-so tells me that I just need to...'

Do some of these comments sound familiar to you? Let's take a look at these one at a time:

I can't ask for help.

Our society generally perpetuates the idea that it is somehow weak or wrong to ask for help. As I have already mentioned, this is not a normal human reaction, but rather a learnt, negative one. I believe this to be major source of continual suffering and ill health. This concept that we just need to keep busy and persevere is a fundamental error. Humans are supposed to support and help one another.

So, ask for what you need, or ask for help even if you don't know exactly what help you need at that moment. The exercise at the end of this chapter will help with that. It really, really is OK to ask for help.

I don't like to put on people.

This is similar to not being able to ask for help. Let's put it this way: if you knew that someone you loved was in terrible distress, would you want to help them? I'm sure you would, and even if you did not immediately know *how* to help them, I am sure you would offer your support nevertheless. Well, that is the exact reason why <u>you</u> should accept help and support from others. People usually want to help, and if they aren't offering, it is probably because they either don't want to impose, or they are in need of help themselves.

Remember, we are socially caring animals, programmed to respond to others' pain. Life is all about giving and taking, and it really is OK to ask for help. Maybe you are someone who has given all your life, or maybe you are someone who doesn't like to give – not particularly out of malice, but just because you prefer to keep yourself to yourself. Either way, if you're grieving, it is your turn to receive. Accept some comfort, some support, some friendship, some silent moments with someone you trust.

To illustrate that support, here is an example from my own life. When I was thirty-five years old, I experienced a massive trauma, which I will describe in detail in a later chapter. Fortunately, my most wonderful sister-in-law was there for me when it happened. She allowed me to stay at the house with her family, she fed me, she listened to my constant crying, comforted me in my numbness, and basically supported me in about every way she could. She continued to do so for a long time. For that support, friendship, and kindness, I shall be forever grateful.

Some twelve years later, she went through a sad break-up with her husband (my brother) and was really struggling. I had never seen her so low, depressed, and lost. I would like to think that I would have been there for her regardless, but remembering back to how she had been so supportive to me all those years ago, I was doubly determined to repay the kindness she had offered me. By that point, I also had some wonderful coping tools, which I knew would help her so much. It was an honour and privilege to be there for her. She certainly found it very difficult to accept help, having been a giver all her life, but finally she could allow herself to receive.

No one can help me. They don't know what I am going through.

This is very different from the aforementioned examples. To the person who feels this way: Firstly, you are right – no one does know what you're going through, as every single person's experiences on this planet is unique to them. However, if you feel no one can help you because they haven't experienced a loss, please let me assure you they can still be there for you. To be blunt, it doesn't matter. IT. DOESN'T. MATTER. Now, don't get me wrong, clearly if someone has been through a loss of any kind, they will have some understanding of what you are going through, but it is not absolutely necessary. Anyone who genuinely cares about you can be a source of support.

So-and-so tells me that I just need to...

It is very interesting that when we lose someone, frequently those around us provide information and advice on how to cope, or tell us what we should and shouldn't be doing. Often, advice from multiple sources can prove contradictory. This so-called 'help' is not too helpful at all, and can become an additional stressor. Loss is an individual experience, and that should be honoured. As a general rule, it is best to avoid anyone who is very opinionated about what you should or shouldn't be doing, as their advice can become overwhelming and confusing.

So, how do you know what help is supportive? We are back to listening to your heart and your intuition. The support you are seeking should be gentle and passive, ideally from someone who is a good listener – someone who will sit quietly and let you vent if you are feeling low or tearful would be perfect. Look for those who are nonjudgemental, who are empathetic, and who truly care about your best interests.

Do you feel there is no support?

My aim in this book is to be inclusive, so that everyone – and I mean *everyone* – reading it can move forward with the ideas and strategies outlined throughout. Let's look at your emotional supporters. Do you have family or friends that could fill this role? Do you have neighbours you feel comfortable with? Do you have work colleagues you could turn to? Do you have acquaintances in groups or clubs you attend? Do you have support networks at work? If you have answered Yes to any of these questions, you are on your way to accessing the help you need.

However, if you feel you have nobody, I want to tell you that within the *Joy Beyond Grief* network and community (which is expanding all the time), you can find support. You can join the *Joy Beyond Grief* Facebook page, where you can communicate with others in situations similar to yourself, or even better, find support from those who have previously benefited from the *Joy Beyond Grief* approach to loss. Additionally, as you go through this chapter, and indeed the book, you will discover various ways to help yourself combat loneliness, and these may open some doors for you in terms of finding help within your immediate family or friends. At the back of the book, there are references to places where you can seek help from people who are familiar with the methods used within the *Joy Beyond Grief* framework, so please check them out, too.

Nature's help

Nature is a wonderful healer, and can certainly be a gentle, soothing source of emotional support, with its immense beauty and diversity providing a constant source of comfort. Perhaps you could go out walking or cycling, and while doing so, I suggest you really try and stay in the moment; try to be mindful. Look all around you at the different trees, flowers, landscapes, etc. Listen to the birds, smell the plants and flowers, touch the leaves. There is so much to take in using all of your senses. By staying aware of what is going on all around you, you are allowing your body to relax and just enjoy the moment for what it is.

Do not underestimate the power of nature as a healer, and do not underestimate the power of trying to stay in the moment – literally, moment by moment. If you are unable to get out for a walk, simply take some time to sit and look out of a window. Even tending to houseplants can help. And if you don't have any, perhaps you could consider going to your local florist to see what they have. There are many studies that show how nature helps reduce anger, fear, stress, and negative emotions, and there is an ever-growing amount of research into nature's association with positive moods and psychological wellbeing.[4,5,6] Go and find some nature, even just for a little while.

Exercise is helpful, too

The benefits of exercise are enormous, and having been a personal trainer for many years, I know that keeping active can help with many negative psychological problems, such as depression, anxiety, and certainly grief. When I was running my own personal training business, I would always say, 'There is a form of exercise for everyone. You just have to find the right one for you.' What exercise do you do? Or fancy having a go at?

If you have always exercised regularly, I urge you to keep it going, even when you really find it difficult to muster the energy. Exercise releases hormones that help lift your spirits. If you have never exercised, please consider trying something – maybe an exercise class or going for a swim. This could provide the added benefit of a new social setting, too. Alternatively, simply go out for a walk with a friend, and you can talk and get the benefits of exercise at the same time. If you can manage it, do try and incorporate some exercise into your day. When you are feeling heartbroken, it is crucial to help that heart of yours, and by literally exercising the heart muscle, you will be helping your body on both a spiritual and emotional level.

Emotional support begins your journey. This book will guide you and support you as if I was sitting with you, in your home as a friend – a fellow connected human being who has already walked the painful path of grief, and who is a little way ahead of you on that path as a result, holding a light to guide you along.

We have begun our journey together, where I will be with you every step of the way. For your first small step, I encourage you to find some support. I also encourage you to start your journaling, which you can use for writing down your feelings and thoughts. You can use it for some of the exercises in this book too.

Below are three exercises that I invite you to try. The first is very simple, yet effective – a wonderful exercise to help you become more heart-focused, calm, and in tune with your whole body. I will encourage you at specific points in this book to practise this exercise.

The second exercise is to answer some questions to help you find support; you can write the answers to them in your journal.

The third exercise I invite you to complete is the chart entitled *The Awareness Heart* from my trio of *Grieving Hearts,* which will help you to focus on specific areas where you may need help from your emotional supporter.

Joy Beyond Grief – Self-Love Exercise

Heart breathing

Sit comfortably in a chair, uncross your legs and allow your body to relax as much as possible. If you prefer, you can do this lying down. Firstly, become aware of your breathing – do not change its rhythm, just focus on your breath for about a minute. Then, take your awareness down to your heart, place both your hands on your heart, and imagine breathing in through your heart, and then breathing out through your heart. Continue this for a few minutes, or however long feels comfortable to you. While doing this, try and focus on a colour that feels right for you in that moment (it may be a different colour every time you do this, and that is fine). Totally immerse yourself in the colour and focus on the heart breathing.

By focusing on your breath and your heart simultaneously, you are helping to build coherence between your heart and brain. This carries numerous benefits, including balancing your emotions, bringing calm to your thoughts, and helping with your mental clarity, which may all have been adversely affected if you have recently suffered bereavement.

It would be beneficial to do this exercise every day, not just to help you focus on this chapter's objective of finding emotional support, but as a tool to generally help you with your grief. For further information regarding developing your heart breathing exercise, please see the *Resources* section.

Feel free to practise this exercise as often as you like. I will also invite you to do this exercise at specific points in the book, to help you reconnect with your heart as a means of continual practice, and at other times because I feel you may need to do it. So, when you see the sign below, please repeat the exercise.

Please note that for some people this breathing exercise– this focusing on the heart – may feel too painful initially. If this is you, then simply focus on your breathing for a few moments without the heart focus.

Please note: heart breathing can be used with children.

Questions on emotional support

Now that you have calmed your heart, allowing for heart/brain cohesion, I invite you to answer the following questions regarding your emotional support. (Remember, the care you are looking for would best be gentle and trusting – quite simply, support which feels right for you.)

1. Do you have support from your immediate family?
2. Do you have support from your extended family?
3. Do you have support from friends, or even acquaintances?
4. Do you belong to any clubs, organisations, or groups, where you could seek individual support?
5. Do you feel that you have no support at all?
6. Do you feel that you do not need any support?

If you answered Yes to any one of the first four questions, the next step is to let that person or those persons know that you would like them to be there for you, and help you during this difficult time. Perhaps you will ask one of them to be your grief buddy, and thus encourage them to engage with you. It would be wonderful to have your grief buddy join you on your journey through this book, completing all of the supportive exercises alongside you.

If you answered Yes to Question 5, please get involved in the *Joy Beyond Grief* community via its Facebook page. Join in with the suggested exercises, and seek the help you need from those referenced at the back of the book.

If you answered Yes to Question 6, I am really glad that you are reading this book, as it will explain why support is so important following loss.

I would strongly ask you to reconsider your view. Loss is a very stressful experience, and support can make such a difference, for all the reasons discussed in this first chapter. Don't face this difficult time alone.

Having now taken your first steps on seeking emotional support and seen how vital that is, the next step is to clarify other aspects of your grieving experience, so that your emotional supporter (grief buddy) can begin to help you.

The Awareness Heart

I invite you to fill in the *Awareness Heart*. I have developed three *Grieving Hearts* in total, but in this chapter, you will only be asked to complete one. As the name suggests, this is a *Heart* which will provide you with insight into some of the general issues that may have been brought about by your loss. This *Heart* should only be completed on a monthly basis, or maybe even at longer intervals, as effecting changes to these circumstances will take time.

There are eight questions to be answered by scoring the intensity of your initial response to them. They start at the inner part of the heart (0), and move outwards to just beyond the heart (+10). Zero indicates a major problem, while +10 means that you feel you are coping well. We will be working towards moving towards the outer heart.

When you're ready, mark each of the eight questions along the line from 0 - +10. If you are unsure about any, just guess (you would be very surprised at how accurate guessing can be for these exercises). Once you have answered each question, please read the information just under the *Awareness Heart*.

THE AWARENESS HEART
Aim to move towards the outer heart
& expansion of your true self

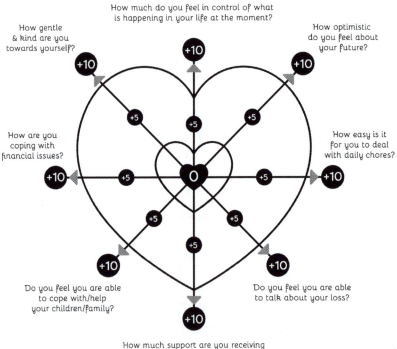

How much do you feel in control of what
is happening in your life at the moment?

How gentle
& kind are you
towards yourself?

How optimistic
do you feel about
your future?

How are you
coping with
financial issues?

How easy is it
for you to deal
with daily chores?

Do you feel you are able
to cope with/help
your children/family?

Do you feel you are able
to talk about your loss?

How much support are you receiving
from family & friends?

The centre of the heart marked 0 indicates you are
not coping very well with this area of your grief.

Moving outwards towards +10 indicates you are coping
better and better with this area of your grief.

20

If you have given any of the eight questions a 5 or below, note that this is an area where you need a lot of support at the moment. Have a chat about your results with your grief buddy, and if it turns out that there is anything they can do to help you immediately, let them help. It may be that they can pay a few bills on your behalf, or it could just be something as simple as sitting and listening to you talk about your loss, or perhaps doing some tidying up around your house. This is a simple, effective way to clarify where you need help, and each of these questions will be addressed in the book, either directly or indirectly.

Chapter 2

FEELINGS AND EMOTIONS: IGNORE OR EMBRACE?

'Feelings are not supposed to be logical. Dangerous
is the man who has rationalised his emotions.'
David Borenstein

'YOU NEED TO KEEP YOURSELF busy ... take your mind off it' is what several well-meaning adults told me when my father died. *Really!?* Keep busy, take my mind off it ... OK, yeah, that makes sense. My father, whom I loved so dearly, who was everything to me, who was no longer there and whom I missed terribly ... I should just keep him out of my mind and get on with things! Well, even if I had wanted to do that (which I didn't), it was impossible, because whenever I was least expecting it, he would pop into my head. Occasionally, it was in the form of happy thoughts about some wonderful moment we had shared, but more often than not, it came in the form of negative feelings, such as the pain of losing him. I would think of him lying in bed all the time, or recall memories from when he actually died. Keep busy? I don't think so. With hindsight, though, I guess that is what actually happened, even if I didn't realise it at the time. I encourage you not to join the Keep Yourself Busy Brigade. It doesn't help, and I shall explain why.

Some six years after my father's death, I got married and we had our first beautiful daughter. Suddenly, there was a *dad* around again, only this time it was my husband. Memories of my own dad – of what happened to him and how awful it was – soon became overwhelming, to the extent that I became very depressed, sad, and full of the same old emotions I had experienced when he died. All that pain came flooding back. I now know what was happening and why, but I didn't at the time. I was constantly being retriggered back into my old, undealt-with grief. Basically, if you do not deal with grief at the time of loss, there is always the potential that it will come back and rear its ugly head when you are least expecting it.

At the time of my daughter's birth, I had no way of predicting that the grief was about to come back. This should have been a time of enormous happiness in my life, but instead it was tainted by that deep depression, which left my poor husband feeling totally confused and helpless. That is how my undealt-with grief manifested. Clearly, not everyone is the same, and that was just my experience – our losses are individual. However, become one of the Keep Yourself Busy Brigade, and the potential for your pain to either never go away, or to come back to haunt you, is increased.

I regularly deal with the consequences of both of these scenarios with my clients. It is simply a form of distraction that causes ongoing pain and suffering. Don't get me wrong: keeping busy is not a problem in and of itself. However, keeping busy as a way to avoid pain is. This form of distraction comes from what we have learnt in life, and these learnings become beliefs (we *believe* that we must avoid pain at all costs). Everything connected to these beliefs becomes engrained in our very being. Our beliefs become our perceptions of the world (the world is full of pain to be avoided), and our world reflects those beliefs back at us (there's pain everywhere – I must avoid it).

Our lives are often defined by our long-standing beliefs, be they conscious or unconscious. If the pain is not dealt with, at some point something will trigger those old painful feelings again, and life will become very difficult to deal with. Two questions are important here. The first is, have you any past grief that was not properly dealt with? And secondly, can you see how important it is to deal with the grief you are experiencing now, so as to avoid such problems reoccurring in the future? Distraction is not a long-term solution for dealing with grief. There is pain in the world (and don't you know it), but there are also healthy ways to deal with it.

Emotions and feelings

Let us briefly differentiate between emotions and feelings.

We often use these two words interchangeably, but they are different. Emotions are hardwired, universal, and have a physiological component. Feelings are our individual reaction to an emotion and provide meaning to an emotional experience. Your emotions give you awareness about your world, whereas your feelings are your conscious awareness of the emotions themselves.

And now, let's look at how this is related to your grieving experience at the moment. Loss can evoke any number of emotions. You may feel sad, lonely, and heartbroken, etc. Specific to you, different aspects of your loss bring up different emotions. Say you are experiencing fear. Your heart rate is elevated, and you're sweating and agitated (an emotion). You realise that you are feeling fearful of the future, wondering what is going to happen to you now, and how you are going to cope (a feeling). The emotion is fear, and you are feeling it in your own personal way. If you can feel and recognise your emotions, life can become a lot easier.

This may sound obvious at first, but with the constant 'emotional ignoring training' that most of us experience sometime in our lives (often starting in childhood), it may not be so easy to recognise your feelings. Remember, emotions and feelings can become disconnected, and this is what gives rise to the Keep Yourself Busy Brigade and the Stiff Upper Lip Club. This disconnect can lead to many problems, so in this chapter I hope to help you to either reconnect with your emotions, or explore them further and understand them fully, ahead of future chapters where I will help you deal with them.

By now, you will have gathered that, from my perspective and experience, to ignore your emotions is not such a clever move. Whether you are pushing emotions away, embracing them, or feeling totally overwhelmed by them, let's move forward and explore the best way to help you acknowledge where you are. This, my friend, is a very good starting point – no judgement on yourself, simply an observation. Remember, looking at your pain in a proactive, gentle way will help your life begin to feel very different. If you need help with this, why not ask your grief buddy to discuss it with you?

Pain shows the depth of love

Bereavement is not about trying to do just anything to avoid the pain. Rather, it is about connecting with that pain and all the emotions that accompany it, and then dealing with them. Constantly trying to push the pain away just makes that pain bigger and bigger, and has the potential to continue for much longer than is necessary. Often, it can burst out in unexpected situations. Believe it or not, the pain and emotions you are experiencing are there for a reason. If we didn't feel pain when someone we love dies, we wouldn't be human, and we certainly wouldn't have cared much for him or her. The perceived separation of loss is a massive part of this, and unless we do something to try and feel reconnected and less separated, we can suffer for a long time with a lot of continual hurting. I will talk about what I mean by 'connection' later in the book.

Trying to push pain away is denying yourself the opportunity to move through your grief in a healthy, more natural way. Don't try to push it away. It won't help and the pain won't go anywhere. You will just push it into the background, where it will linger and pop out when you are least expecting it. Pain is there in grieving terms so that we know we have lost someone very dear to us, and I feel that pushing pain away as opposed to honouring it is a major problem in our society. The depth of your pain is a reflection of the depth of your love. I invite you to use that depth of love to help you through your pain. That is the ultimate aim of this book.

Please take some time to heart breathe now.

Identifying and acknowledging your emotions is a crucial first step in helping to heal the pain of grief. When you are truly connected with your emotional self, you are able to cope much better and deal with all aspects of your loss. The key to helping yourself and allowing those around you to help you is, without question, about you understanding your emotional state, being honest about it, and fully embracing it. If you don't, it will be very difficult to function at all, let alone deal with any other aspects of your life that needs to be taken care of.

What are our emotions all about?

When I was studying for my undergraduate degree in Psychology, I chose to take a module focused on emotions, and it became apparent very quickly that this was quite a controversial and rather confused topic. Even the psychologists researching in this area couldn't agree on how many emotions actually existed. Some only acknowledged two: love and fear, whereas others recognised well over forty. Although various theories and ideas about emotions have been researched extensively, there is still no general consensus as to their meaning. There is also great discussion on whether emotions should be labelled *positive* or *negative*. I do not want to get into that discussion here, but for reading ease throughout this book, I will refer to emotions generally as *negative* or *positive*.

Emotions comprise a unique and perfectly designed guiding system, there to alert us to what is going on, both in our internal and external world. If you are experiencing negative emotions, that's because they are trying to tell you that something is wrong, and conversely, if you are experiencing positive emotions, they are reassuring you that all is well. These are vital components of your wellbeing, crucial to your ability to navigate through this life with all of its varied experiences. Although we can't just change those negative feelings with a click of the fingers, what we can do is soften them, and then understand them. However, the main aim in this book is to go one step further, and ultimately transform them into feelings of peace and even joy.

To reiterate, negative emotions show something is wrong, and positive emotions show that things are going well. It is both as simple as that and as complicated as that. What do I mean? Well, it is simple, because it is pretty clear that when you lose a loved one, you are going to feel full of negative emotions, such as sadness, loneliness, and pain or even depression. Clearly, we do not all feel exactly the same feelings; however, we are all the same in that how we feel is our guide: if we are feeling good, things in our lives are as we wish them to be, or if we are feeling bad, they are not as we would like them to be. Simple, yes?

And as I said above, our emotions are also complicated, because often – and this is primarily the case in Western society – we are encouraged A) not to show our emotions, and B) to disconnect from them. As I mentioned earlier, this can be a particular problem for men (I know that I am generalising here, as women can have the same issues, too), who have been brought up to hide, ignore, suppress, and totally deny that they have any emotions at all!

People are often criticised for being 'too sensitive' when expressing their emotions, but really, why must we continually try to deny this natural aspect of ourselves? It seriously is not a clever move. In my opinion, this viewpoint is outdated and totally incorrect. Our emotions, and our expression of them through feelings, are crucial to our physical health and mental wellbeing, and are fundamental to who we are. Many people working within energy psychology, medicine, academia, and various research institutes around the world also hold this same opinion.

> 'If you trust and attend to your emotions,
> they'll take care of you. If you don't,
> your life will be pretty miserable.'
> Karla McLaren

This quote is taken from the excellent book *The Language of Emotions*, and really says it how it is.[1] Are you trusting and attending to your emotions during this difficult time? If the answer is No, fear not. We shall journey this emotional road together. Incidentally, Karla's book goes into great detail about individual emotions, should you wish to analyse them further. I decided that in this book, it would not be necessary, as my aim is for you to acknowledge, recognise, and simply name your emotions and feelings for what they mean personally to you, and then to move through them in a gentle way.

Attending to your emotions is crucial, but what I am not saying is that we should go around expressing our emotions when we are not in a safe environment to do so. It is good to know when to express our emotions and when not to. That is why the first chapter makes clear that it is crucial to have that safe space in which to express how you are feeling.

When we try to hide or deny our feelings for long periods of time, two things happen. Firstly, we become confused. We may feel something, and having been warned against this, we try and suppress the feeling, which in turn leads to anything from mild anxiety to total self-hatred. Secondly, we begin to lose sight of who we really are, because we are not being true to ourselves or what we really feel. This leads to a distorted view of what we want in life and where we want to be. Basically, we become distanced from our intuition, our heart's guidance, and what makes our heart sing, or as some would say, distanced from our 'spirit' or 'soul'. (This is discussed at length in later chapters.)

Let's explore this by understanding and acknowledging where you are with your emotions. I invite you to ask yourself the following questions in a self-discovering exercise (you can just answer Yes or No in your journal, but if you expand on your answers, you'll have greater insights).

1. Are you trying to push away how you are feeling?
2. Are you saying to people that you are OK when you are not?
3. Are you trying to kid yourself about how you are really feeling?
4. Are you keeping as busy as you can because you fear that if you stop, the pain will catch up with you?
5. Are you doing anything just to avoid feeling something?
6. Do you play down exactly how much pain you are feeling to other people?
7. Do you sometimes burst out with anger, and then find that you don't know where it has come from?

If you have answered Yes to any of the above questions, it means that to some degree you are suppressing your emotions. Believe me, you are not alone in this. However, for all the reasons I have previously mentioned, I invite you to be open to change, to engage in the exercises provided in this book, and to keep an open mind.

Having answered the above questions, here are some more questions.

1. Do you find it easy to express your feelings?
2. When your loss overwhelms you emotionally, are you able to ask for help?
3. Do your friends regard you as emotional?
4. Are you allowing yourself space to acknowledge your feelings as and when they arise?
5. Are you being honest with yourself about how you are feeling?
6. Do you openly share and talk about how you feel?
7. Are you able to say that you just can't do something on a specific day, as it is all getting too much for you?

If you have answered Yes to any of these questions, you are to some extent in touch with how you are feeling, and are able to express those feelings. The more Yes answers, the more emotionally open you are. Please remember that this is about finding out where you are: it is not a competition, nor is it a judgement. Wherever you happen to be is absolutely fine, but if you don't know where you are, how can things move at all? Whatever your answers revealed, this book will help – and at the end of this chapter you will be shown a tool that will help you enormously with where you are emotionally.

It is really important to know that by actually exploring, accepting, and owning your feelings, you are not going to intensify them – quite the reverse. Taking action will help to lower their intensity, and subsequently their negative effects on you and your health. Until you fully acknowledge and accept how you are feeling in any given moment, you cannot change how you react. Try not to be afraid, and be open to the possibility that there may be a different way to 'do feelings' than what you've been led to believe. Later on, I will show you a gentle and effective tool to help with emotional intensity.

Do I feel or think my emotions?

What is the difference between our emotions/feelings and thoughts? This differentiation is very important. It may seem obvious to say that feelings and emotions are supposed to be felt, while thoughts are supposed to be thought. However, in reality what so often happens is that we try and think our way out of a feeling. Just reflect on that for a moment. We try and *think* our way out of a *feeling*. Not only do I believe that this is another huge problem in society, but I also believe that it is not possible, and yet this is exactly what most people are trying to do most of the time. Why?

We are taught at an early age to use our brains for everything and, as mentioned before, to ignore our emotions. I don't remember being at school and having any lessons in Intuition, or How to Follow your Heart, or Experiencing your Emotions. That is because there weren't any, and there still aren't today! We are back to that old 'keep yourself busy' thing. 'Think about something else', or 'Do something to take your mind off it'. That last comment really shows the extent to which, as a society, we believe we can control our emotions with our brains.

From the time when we are very young (and impressionable), we are taught to think, think, think. Throughout our school years, we learn to think our way through maths problems, think what we are going to write in that essay, think about which king or queen of England (If you are in England) followed which other one, think, think, think! Education is totally geared towards thinking, not feeling. No wonder our emotional intelligence is such unknown territory.

In many aspects of our lives, thinking is totally the appropriate and essential tool for the job. We obviously need to think about what time we are getting up in the morning to go to work, and what we are going to cook for dinner. In our loss, we need to think about funeral arrangements, and what we are going to do about the mortgage, etc., but (and here is the *BIG* but) it is not our only way of resolving the issues that we are confronted with. It is not our only option for coping with our lives and what happens in them.

For example, I worked with a client, Angela, who felt incredibly guilty about something she had said to her partner before he died. She kept that guilt constantly running through her head, 'Why did I say ... If only I hadn't said it ...' – thinking, thinking, thinking. She kept beating herself up for saying what she said. Was that in any way helping her? Obviously not. The guilt she was feeling made her go over and over in her head why she said what she said. She was trying to think her way out of that feeling so that she could resolve her guilt, but her guilt was where the problem lay, and that was simply a feeling.

Constantly thinking about what had happened achieved nothing positive whatsoever. In fact, it achieved absolutely *nothing at all,* and just kept making her feel worse and worse. Her partner had passed away, so how could she possibly think her way out of it? He was gone. But what if she had been able to deal with the emotion of guilt? Do you think she would have had the same thoughts occurring over and over? If she no longer felt guilty, do you believe she would still have those thoughts going around and around her head? I will return to Angela in a while.

By constantly running something over and over in your mind, you risk driving yourself mad, and it will not help to resolve the issue. It causes you to feel a lack of control over your situation, and often only results in making you feel even worse. It can seem like the feeling will never go away, and indeed, in many cases people suffer with these feelings year upon year. You simply cannot think your way out of a feeling.

Your brain is trying to find a reason why, and your rational mind is trying to find justification for this feeling while looking for a practical way out, but this is not going to help much at all. Trying to use your rational mind, also known as your conscious mind, to help yourself through negative emotions is like trying to bang in a nail with a paintbrush! Wrong tool for the job! Feelings do not always appear logical or rational, and so therefore, trying to resolve them by using logical thinking isn't going to work. Trying to use your brain to feel better is the wrong tool for the job, period. Here again is that quote used at the beginning of this chapter. Please reflect on it:

'Feelings are not supposed to be logical. Dangerous
is the man who has rationalised his emotions.'
David Borenstein

A brief look at the conscious and subconscious mind

First of all, there is the *conscious mind*, which is rational, and adept at dealing with regular matters on a daily basis, such as your awareness at this very moment while reading this book.

Then, you have the *subconscious mind*, which we will be working with in this book. This is responsible for your involuntary actions, such as breathing, as well as your innate, habitual responses. It is the storehouse for all of your memories, beliefs, values, and feelings of identity.

Here is a simple exercise to show the difference between the conscious mind and the subconscious mind. Think about your breathing and begin to control it, taking deep breaths in and out. Here, your conscious mind is in charge. Now, stop controlling it and let it flow naturally. Focus on something else in the room for a second and then come back to your breathing, and it's clear that your subconscious has been handling it all while you've been elsewhere. While your conscious mind only accesses 10 per cent of your mental processing and is voluntary, your subconscious is in control of the remaining 90 per cent of your mental potential and is generally inaccessible to your awareness. Basically, when you are not consciously aware of something your subconscious will take over.

So, we would all do well to understand the subconscious a little better. (See illustration below.) Remember, when you are trying to think your way out of your feelings, you are trying to use that 10 per cent to do a job that it isn't even designed for. However, if we look at what is happening on a subconscious level – where the emotions are triggered – we are able to make some profound changes that will subsequently have a major impact on the pain of loss.

THE CONSCIOUS
AND SUBCONSCIOUS MIND

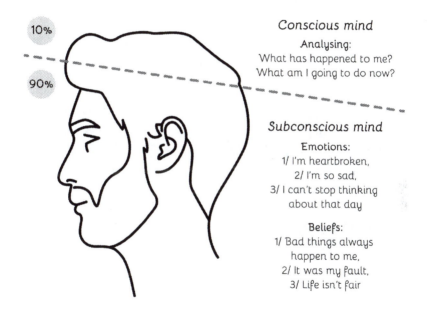

10%

90%

Conscious mind
Analysing:
What has happened to me?
What am I going to do now?

Subconscious mind
Emotions:
1/ I'm heartbroken,
2/ I'm so sad,
3/ I can't stop thinking
about that day

Beliefs:
1/ Bad things always
happen to me,
2/ It was my fault,
3/ Life isn't fair

The more we try to use that 10 per cent, the more we get frustrated with the lack of results, and then point the finger at our willpower, which is part of our conscious mind. Let me tell you something: you can have as much willpower as you can carry – bucketloads of the stuff – but if something is in your subconscious mind, no amount of willpower will shift it, so stop trying to power through. It's yet another example of the wrong tool for the job. You cannot change what is in your subconscious mind with your conscious mind alone.

So, the question is, what is in your subconscious? Your interpretation of emotions in terms of feelings, beliefs, and habits is what is in your subconscious, and it will be affected by, and is affecting, your grieving experience. Luckily, there are tools to help with whatever is in your subconscious mind that is not supporting you and we have our wonderful heart intuition to help too. We will explore this much more later, but for now, keep doing your heart breathing exercise, as this is part of the healing process.

> 'Until you make the unconscious conscious, it
> will direct your life and you will call it fate.'
> Carl Jung

Let's return to Angela, who was trying to use her conscious mind to find relief from her guilt. She and I worked with her subconscious mind to alleviate the hurt it was causing her, and she was soon able to let that feeling go. Over time, the memory began to feel totally different, and was no longer going around and around in her head. In fact, about two weeks after we worked on this issue, I asked her if she was still affected by it in any way, and she actually had trouble recalling the memory at all. This was in complete contrast to the way she had been feeling for a long period previously.

Everything we did is explained in this book. At the end of this chapter, this new way of dealing with how you are feeling begins, gently and in a doable way. However, before I reveal your first tool, I must first address my final point in this chapter: your emotional past.

What's in your emotional past?

Everyone comes into their grieving experience from a different perspective. Your life before your loss will have a significant effect on your grieving experience. Before you lost your loved one, what was happening in your life?

Were you happy? Was your life just as you had always wanted it? Were you stressed because of work, or had you been having relationship problems? We do not experience grief in a vacuum. At the time we experience loss, we are living our lives in our own very individual and unique way, with all its joys and woes.

Let us delve a little deeper. When we are born, we are totally connected with our emotions. We have had no social conditioning. If we want food, a cuddle or a drink, we cry – a clear outward expression that something is wrong. We need something that we do not have. We openly express our emotions and needs. However, as we age, our learning experiences heavily influence how we act, and for some people this can occur very early in life.

If your environment is unsafe, you learn to act accordingly. If, as a baby, you experience negative responses to your cries, you may end up suppressing these natural responses, and this will have an effect on the emotional responses you exhibit as an adult.

Our childhood experiences have a massive impact on what we believe in, how we act and behave, and how we deal with our emotions. We may learn not to show emotions, believing it to be a sign of weakness. We may learn that being quiet is the only way to be safe. We may learn that we only get attention when we are ill. I could go on and on, but I'm sure you get the picture. These early learning experiences, along with those that we gain as our lives progress, shape us, and often lead us to a point where we are still affected by them long after we have forgotten how they started. And guess which part of our mind deals with all this? You got it: the subconscious.

'The subconscious mind is a repository of stimulus-response tapes derived from instincts and learned experiences,' says famous cell biologist, Bruce Lipton.[2] He goes on to explain, 'The subconscious mind is strictly habitual; it will play the same behavioural responses to life's signals over and over again.'[3] We have experiences in life, and we learn how to respond to those experiences through our subconscious. Thus, any hint of a similar experience will naturally illicit a similar response. (Please read Bruce Lipton's work, or even better, watch him on YouTube. He is very knowledgeable and charismatic. I totally recommend his book, *The Biology of Belief*.)

Ever had the feeling 'Why am I doing this again?' 'Why does that keep happening to me?' or 'Why do I always feel like ...?' It is because your subconscious mind is acting habitually from what it learnt early in life, and now something is retriggering it. Interesting, but what does this have to do with your grieving experience? A lot, actually. When you lost your loved one, you weren't a blank slate – you experienced it from your own unique, individual perspective on life. With your own sets of learnings, beliefs, thoughts, and behaviours that have all developed at their own rate. Hence, everyone grieves differently.

You may be experiencing one emotion far more than any other because that particular emotion is one which is oh-so-familiar to you. Let's use anger as an example here. You may be feeling a great deal of anger about any number of aspects of your loss. This anger may be more prominent than any other emotion. It may be that anger has played a significant role in your life, and your loss has now amplified it. You are likely experiencing a whole array of emotions, but if anger has been a significant emotion in your life, the shock and trauma of loss could exacerbate it further. I use anger here, but any of the emotions that seem to be reoccurring throughout your grieving experience are just as relevant. We will all have our own prominent emotions, and these will affect how we experience grief.

Did you just do the heart breathing exercise, or did you skip it? Come on, do it! It is these small steps that will make the difference.

Now, begin to think about which emotions are most prevalent for you in your loss. Had they played a key role in your life before your loss? Recognising familiar emotions is what makes our grieving experience so individual, and working with those emotions is in my opinion the most helpful way to manoeuvre through your loss.

Historically, grief has been seen in stages with Elizabeth Kübler-Ross's five stages of grief, denial, bargaining, depression and acceptance being at the forefront of many grief counsellors' strategies to help with grief. Those of us who work with grief owe, I feel, a great debt to this lady – particularly in understanding that there is a process to grief. However, whilst I have great respect for the work she did, I feel things have moved on: working with individuals with their own unique grieving process is how I work with clients now.

Before you begin the self-love exercises in this chapter, let's summarise. We are emotional beings, and it is natural to be emotional, especially when we have lost a loved one. You are going to feel many intense and diverse emotions, but please be assured that your grieving process will really be helped along if you recognise, accept, and own how you are feeling. Trying to keep busy, or trying to think your way out of feelings related to any aspect of your loss, is not going to help you. It will just send you around and around in circles, exhausting you and making you feel even worse. As you read this book, help yourself to move through your grief at your own pace, gently and with kindness to yourself. The many tools found here allow for that to occur one small step at a time.

I have achieved peace and lots more, and so have many of my clients. You can do it, too. It may well feel like an enormous mountain to climb, and I understand if it seems an impossible task at this moment, but that is only because you don't have all that mountaineering equipment to hand. You will have by the end of this book, though. Trust me.

Joy Beyond Grief – Self-Love Exercises

The Grieving Hearts

In chapter 1, you were introduced to the *Awareness Heart,* which hopefully helped you clarify the areas of your life in which you may need some support. Some of those issues might also have provided you with insight into specific emotions that you are experiencing. I invite you to use the next two *Grieving Hearts:* the *Healing Heart* and the *Transformational Heart* to help focus on how you are feeling – to help recognise your emotional state, and to give clarity as to where you are at this very moment in time. If you register your email address at my website (www.janicethompson.co.uk), you can download these *Grieving Hearts* in the form of a workbook.

Firstly, let's look at the *Healing Heart.* You will need to identify up to eight of the most prominent emotions you are experiencing. Below are some emotions to help you distinguish and isolate those which are most relevant to you, but they are only suggestions. Please select the right words for you. Also, and very importantly, you can add feelings like 'This horrible feeling in my chest', 'This aching in my heart' and 'This lump in my stomach'. They don't have to be one-word answers.

---

angry, annoyed, anxious, ashamed, bitter, broken, chaotic, cold, confused, defeated, depressed, deserted, desperate, detached, disconnected, disgust, disheartened, drained, dread, empty, fragile, frightened, furious, guilty, hopeless, helpless, impulsive, insecure, irresponsible, isolated, lonely, lost, mad, miserable, out of control, overwhelmed, panicked, paranoid, punished, rage, rejected, resentful, responsible, sad, self-destructive, shut down, unhappy, untrusting, unsupported, worn out, worried

---

Here is an example.

THE HEALING HEART EXAMPLE
Aim to move towards the inner heart & nearer your true self

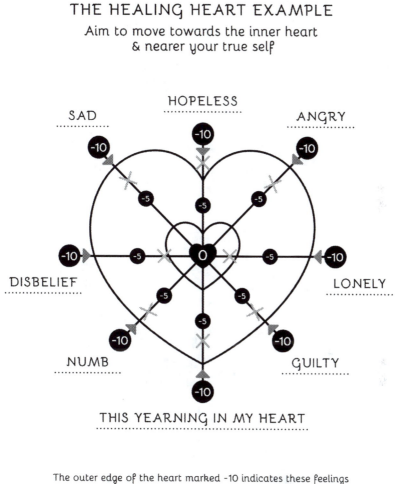

The outer edge of the heart marked -10 indicates these feelings are strong and possibly debilitating for you.

Moving inwards towards 0 indicates that your feelings are becoming milder and milder/are lessening in strength.

Below is an empty *Healing Heart* for you to fill in. Once you have added in your main eight emotions/feelings, the next step is to give each of them an intensity score, ranging from -10 to 0, where -10 is the maximum intensity you are feeling, and 0 the least. In the example above, the intensities were marked with a cross. You can use a cross to rate your intensity or find your own sign. Please don't get too hung up on this. A rough estimate is fine, and if you find it difficult to do, simply guess. As I mentioned before, guessing is remarkably accurate.

YOUR HEALING HEART
Aim to move towards the inner heart
& nearer your true self

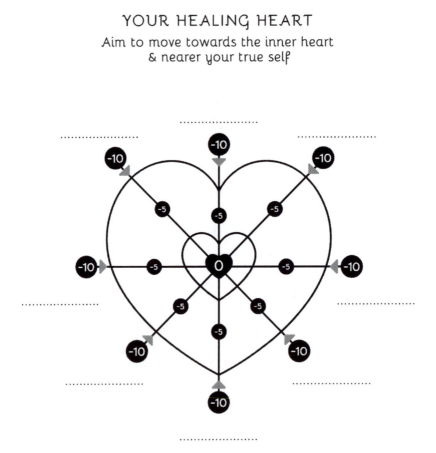

The outer edge of the heart marked -10 indicates these feelings are strong and possibly debilitating for you.

Moving inwards towards 0 indicates that your feelings are becoming milder and milder/are lessening in strength.

Now we shall look at the *Transformational Heart*. You will again need to identify up to eight of the most prominent emotions you are experiencing. Below are some emotions to help you distinguish and isolate which are most relevant to you, but they are only suggestions. Please select the right words for you. Also, and very importantly, you can add feelings like 'This calm in my mind', 'This appreciation in my heart', or 'This warmth in my tummy'. They don't have to be one-word answers.

accepting, adaptable, at ease, authentic, awake, balanced, beautiful, blessed, blissful, bonded, calm, capable, centred, cheerful, confident, content, courageous, creative, comfortable, connected, decisive, dignified, elated, energetic, empowered, enthusiastic, focused, gracious, grateful, grounded, happy, inspired, joyful, loved, loving, optimistic, passionate, peaceful, powerful, proud, purposeful, self-accepting, serene, stable, supported, thankful, trusting, worthy

It is probably easier for you to fill in the *Healing Heart* at the moment, but it is important to complete this chart, so that you have some perspective on where you are going – or at least to acknowledge any small positives in your life at the moment. If you can't get eight emotions, just do as many as you can. Below are four ideas to help you fill in this *Transformational Heart*:

1/ You may have noticed some small things that happen in your day which lift your heart a little. Think how they made you feel, and channel those emotions here.

2/ You could look for emotions that are the opposite of the words you used in the *Healing Heart*.

3/ You could think back to a time when something good was happening in your life, and use the emotions embedded in that memory to inspire you.

4/ You could simply choose the positive emotions that you would like to feel at some point in your journey. The main thing is to be honest with yourself, as this will be the most helpful thing for you on your healing journey.

Here is an example, followed by an empty chart for you to fill in.

THE TRANSFORMATIONAL HEART EXAMPLE
Aim to move towards the outer heart
& expansion of your true self

CALM

CONNECTED   JOYFUL

+10   +10

+10

+5   +5   +5

0

+10   +5   +5   +10

AT PEACE   ENERGETIC

+5   +5

+5

+10   +10

CONTENTED   A SOFTNESS IN MY HEART

+10

EMPOWERED

The centre of the heart marked 0 indicates these feelings are mild,
not very strong for you.

Moving outwards towards +10 indicates that your feelings are becoming
stronger and stronger and can be a positive help for you.

Once you have filled in the *Transformational Heart* with your main eight emotions, the next step is to give each of these an intensity score, ranging from 0 to +10, where 0 represents the least amount of intensity that you are feeling, and +10 is the maximum. In the example above, you can see the intensity marked with a cross. Again, use a cross or your own sign. And, as

I said before, don't get too hung up on this; just a rough idea is fine, and if you find it difficult to do, simply guess the intensity.

YOUR TRANSFORMATIONAL HEART
Aim to move towards the outer heart & expansion of your true self

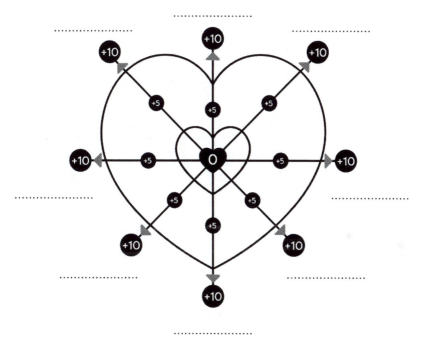

The centre of the heart marked 0 indicates these feelings are mild, not very strong for you.

Moving outwards towards +10 indicates that your feelings are becoming stronger and stronger and can be a positive help for you.

You will have noticed that the scales for the *Healing Heart* and the *Transformational Heart* are different. This really wasn't to confuse you! The reason was to show you the bigger picture (which you can see in the scale below more clearly). The *Healing Heart* scales (more negative emotions) start at -10, and as they decrease in intensity, they move up to 0, and a more neutral place in terms of potential impact.

The *Transformational Heart* scales (more positive emotions) start at +1, and move up to +10 in terms of intensity. So, we are aiming to move towards the right of the scale shown below. This is certainly not a straightforward process, as no one is going to move from left to right and stay there. Life will always be moving back and forth between these two end points, but hopefully it will give you a sense of change as you move through your grieving experience.

THE GRIEF SCALE

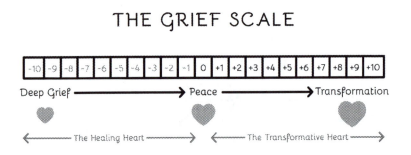

Having completed both of the *Grieving Hearts*, you now have a tangible awareness of where you are emotionally at this moment. With awareness comes change. It can lead to acceptance, and can also allow for positive change. Being aware of how your loss has made you feel is the next step towards helping yourself at this difficult time.

I invite you to rate how intensely you are experiencing the <u>emotions you recorded</u> at regular intervals, preferably weekly. By doing this relatively simple task, I can assure you that you will be moving through your grief towards healing.

For now, just completing the *Grieving Hearts* is all you need to do; but as you progress through this book, you will be coming back to them, so keep them handy. Tools in later chapters will help you with lowering the emotional intensity of the more negative emotions and raising the intensities of the more positive emotions. For now, simply acknowledge and honour any emotions that you are feeling, and respect how you are feeling at any given moment. By acknowledging and rating your emotions on a regular basis, you are helping yourself to begin the process of healing. And that is a significant move in the right direction. Below are a few more reasons for completing these *Grieving Hearts:*

- To help give you clarity as to where you are at this moment in time
- To recognise and *own* your feelings
- To really understand what you are feeling
- To honour and respect where you are at this moment
- To help you to accept where you are
- To give you a way of seeing change in your life
- To identify feelings/emotions you would like to move towards or away from
- To use as a tool to help with your emotional and physical wellbeing
- To help give you a sense of control and empowerment
- Completing them means that you have taken another step towards healing.

Chapter 3

THE SHOCK OF LOSS

'Just as the body goes into shock after physical
trauma, so does the human psyche go into
shock after the impact of a major loss.'
Anne Grant

IT WAS A COOL, CALM summer's evening. I rushed home from the exercise class that I taught to get back to my family. I put the dinner on – spaghetti bolognaise, a family favourite – while Andy, my husband, who had just finished mowing the lawn, sat in the garden talking to our youngest daughter (aged seven at the time), and my eldest daughter did teenager things in her bedroom. Life was good. After several years of commuting, which had been difficult for all the family, Andy had recently transferred from a job in London to local employment – we were looking forward to our first summer together for several years.

I was just getting ready to dish up dinner when my youngest daughter came rushing in from outside, saying that Daddy had collapsed. She thought he was messing around at first, but then she got frightened after realising that something was wrong. I was convinced he was fooling around, as he so often did, but, playing along with the game, I followed her outside. Once in the garden, I very quickly saw this was not a joke. I found my husband on the concrete struggling to breathe, with blood pouring out of his nose from where he had hit the ground after falling from his seat. Looking back, I realise that I went into shock at that point.

I knew instinctively to just get to the phone and call an ambulance. I then called my brother, who lived around the corner, and my eldest daughter fetched our friend and neighbour. Our two dogs were running around like crazy. I was trying to think straight, to help my husband as best I could, but this was extremely difficult. I remember that, as our neighbour and I were crouching next to him, I became obsessed with protecting him from the cold concrete and tried to put a pillow under his head. He had stopped breathing, so I tried to do mouth-to-mouth. He wasn't responding, and when the ambulance arrived, I just got my two daughters together and moved to the other side of the garden. I think I was too frightened to watch as they tried to help him. I cannot thank the emergency services enough for their efforts; I also thank the brilliant doctor who turned up as part of a rapid response team. However, there was unfortunately nothing that they could do.

My husband had had a massive heart attack and passed away on 19 June 2002. No symptoms at all. No signs of any pre-existing health problems. In fact, he had only recently had a medical examination, as part of his job transfer. No time for a goodbye. No time for a simple 'I love you' to be exchanged. He was, quite literally, there one minute and then gone the next. That evening, I lost my beautiful husband, best friend, and soulmate. My two daughters lost their father. Life felt like it would never be the same again, and it wasn't. The very person I needed to help me through this horrendous ordeal was the very man I had just lost. I fell into a state of shock that would affect my whole being. The same was true of my children.

The shock of loss

I now understand the impact of that shock on both my body and my emotional state, and this is why I have dedicated a whole chapter to the shock of loss.

The sudden death of my husband was an immense shock, and if you have lost a loved one in this way, I am sure that you are fully aware of what I'm talking about. It may not be as clear-cut if you lost your loved one in another way, but in my professional experience, there tends to be at least one shock with every loss. The question is more *when*, rather than *if*. If you have lost someone after a long illness, that shock point may not be so obvious. For example, if a close relation is diagnosed with terminal cancer, you will almost certainly experience a shock at the point when you are given the news. If someone you know has been rushed into hospital, and you have then been told that they are not going to make it, that will be a shock point. A phone call in the middle of the night, telling you that someone you love has died, will absolutely be a shock point.

Why is the shock point so important? Because the shock of bereavement will have a significant impact on your body, and failure to deal with it carries the potential for long-term problems.

Let me explain a little more about shock. I am going to take you on a journey, a journey of what happens to the body at the moment a shock occurs, and the associated potential problems. Please do not be alarmed. I am fully aware of the fact that you may well be feeling as though this is the least of your worries at the moment, and that you have enough to deal with. However, it is an aspect of your loss that you would benefit from working with as soon as you are able to. In my opinion, shock is a crucial aspect of loss, and how to deal with it will be clearly explained later in the book. For now, let's look at the impact of a shock to the body.

Run away or fight your loss?

What happens when you experience a shock? I am sure you have heard of the natural responses 'Fight or Flight' – primitive reactions to stress. These are reactions that we still experience today, albeit due to different stressors, and therein lies the problem. Primitive man's stressors came primarily in the form of physical danger, whereas our modern-day stressors predominately come in the form of emotional and psychological problems. For example, our primitive ancestors might have experienced a stress such as being chased by a tiger, and in response they would have either tried to run away (Flight), or they would have stood their ground and tried to kill it (Fight). This would be an extremely physical reaction to an immediate physical threat. On a physiological level, stress hormones such as adrenaline and cortisol would flood their bodies, to enable them to have all the energy that they could muster in order to deal with this potentially life-threatening situation. At the same time, systems such as their digestive system would shut down, as this would not be a priority. We don't need to be digesting food when we are trying to run away from being something else's food.

Today, our body's physiological reactions to stress are the same as our primitive ancestors', with one crucial difference: the causes of that stress. Today's stressors may include losing a job, dealing with debt, coping with deadlines, financial problems, and issues around losing a loved one, or experiencing any other form of loss. Modern-day ways of dealing with loss (particularly in the West) are very different from primitive ways of dealing with loss. However, our bodies still react in the same physical way as our ancestors' bodies did. You may actually be experiencing this at the moment. Bereavement can make you feel like running away, or you may have such strong feelings of anger that you want to blame, shout, and fight someone over what has happened. You may experience those stressors, but you do not utilise the hormones pumping around your body, because you don't actually run away or fight someone. Over time, this has the potential to cause a number of health issues, including an increased risk of chronic heart disease, a compromised immune system, an increased risk of stroke, depression, and a higher risk of heart attack. These are well-documented. (Please see the *Resources* section for links to some of these studies.) So, the combination of your stressors in life, coupled with your loss, could easily be setting you up for the straw that breaks the camel's back, so to speak.

Frozen loss

As well as the fight or flight response to stress, there is another response that is not so well-documented, yet is central to the shock of loss. It is called the 'Freeze' response. Your whole body literally freezes your emotions, and whatever your senses were aware of in that moment will freeze, too. It can simply feel like being frozen to the spot.

Perhaps the best way to understand this is to give an example. A client, whom I'll call Louise, was called to the phone, to be told of her loved one's passing. She was standing in her lounge by the settee, and she picked the phone up from a small table beside her. She had an apple in her hand, as she was just about to eat it when the phone rang. The television was on, with her usual morning programme showing. She was looking out of her window as a teenager cycled past on his bike. She could smell the hot soup on the hob in the kitchen as it was simmering away. When she was told of what had happened on the phone, she froze, and everything within her spatial awareness at that moment froze with her, and was locked into her subconscious mind. All the things she could see, hear, smell, and touch froze with her. This next illustration shows just how many things from that point on had the potential to trigger her in the future. She developed an allergy to apples, and seeing someone cycle would upset her for some time afterwards, although she did not make the connection to start with.

SCENE ILLUSTRATING POTENTIAL TRIGGERS

This is why people can develop phobias and allergies, and why certain smells and sights can upset them in ways that they don't understand. However, when you realise how this freeze response works, you can begin to make those connections. We resolved Louise's freeze response by using methods described later on.

Your shock and subsequent freeze response have two major effects on your body. The first is that huge amounts of information are frozen at the moment of shock, with possible ongoing consequences. The second, and obviously interrelated, is that an enormous amount of energy is produced.

Frozen information

What happens to all this stored information? Well, your body is such a brilliant piece of nature's engineering that it uses the information to alert you to any future potential shocks. You see, your subconscious, where this information is stored, is about survival and protection, and following the massive impact of loss, it recognises any one of those pieces of frozen information as a potential problem to be avoided at all costs. Primitively speaking, this information is held as a matter of life or death. Are you in danger? Are you about to die, too? That is what your subconscious is thinking. If this is the case, and you can't run or fight, which is difficult with loss, the freeze response occurs with its full sensory recording of that moment.

Think about how when an animal feels cornered, it plays dead. This is the freeze response. If it survives, all the information at the time of the shock about where it happened, what time of day it was, what the animal was doing, etc., would be extremely helpful to avoid the situation again. For humans, it all goes straight into the subconscious, which is capable of processing 20,000,000 pieces of information per second, dwarfing the capacity of the conscious mind, which is only capable of processing 40 pieces of information per second.[1]

Each one of those pieces of information in the subconscious has the potential to impact our lives, if the shock isn't dealt with. How? By being potential triggers in the future. Those original feelings and thoughts can resurface and come flooding back just as you originally experienced them. Not only can this be very distressing – it can be extremely confusing as these feelings and thoughts seem to have come out of nowhere.

If you choose to do what the majority of the population do and just keep ploughing on, trying to 'put everything behind you', becoming one of the Keep Yourself Busy Brigade, these old, negative, familiar feelings will just keep repeating themselves over and over when an occasion retriggers them. This is because those stuck emotions don't go away – they stay stuck until you clear them. It may not seem immediately apparent, because as time goes by you learn to accept what has happened, but your subconscious mind will remember.

Have you ever been to a funeral and noticed someone there who doesn't know the deceased very well, but is in floods of tears and is completely inconsolable? This is an example of them being retriggered, probably from a previous loss of someone close to them, or from an aspect of that loss (a piece of the recalled information) which they have not dealt with.

I will explain just how this happened to me further on in the book. I have seen it with many of my clients too. It is heartbreaking to see someone struggling for years, often not knowing why, or attributing it to something totally unrelated. Clearing the stuck energy could give you back a life that is much more peaceful and joyful. It can help you avoid many years of unnecessary suffering. Dealing with it is never as bad as you think it is going to be – nowhere near, actually.

If you now recognise that you may have stuck energy around a shock, fear not. We will be dealing with that.

The energy in a freeze response

The second aspect of the freeze response is the massive amount of energy it produces. This energy needs to be discharged to enable the body's energy system to come back into balance and equilibrium. If the body cannot discharge this energy, it can result in a negative impact. Specific memories may be constantly recalled; numerous physical health issues can occur. We can quite literally get stuck with the pain of that moment, and if not dealt with, it can lead us into prolonged grief and suffering.

The shock of losing someone affects you on many levels: energetically, mentally, physically, and emotionally. However, the effects on the mental, physical, and emotional levels all have their origins in the energetic level.[2] So, it makes sense to deal with shock at the energy level, as this will then have an effect on all of the other levels. Look at your body's energy system as the master system, affecting and being affected by the other body systems.

In chapter 5, we will go into greater detail about the body's energy system, and I will give an example of exactly how the body can release this trapped energy. Animals in their natural environment will shake profusely after being chased by a predator – if they are lucky enough to escape! That is an example of a release of energy after a shock. Unfortunately, humans appear to have lost connection to this automatic response. For further information on this release of energy, please see the reference to Robert Scaer's work in the *Resources* section.

An unexpected, dramatic, isolating, no-strategy-to-deal-with event

META-Health is a new way of understanding ourselves: it incorporates the interconnection of mind, body, and social health, addressing specific situations that can cause a shock and looking at related health issues. I will discuss it in more detail in a later chapter; but what is interesting for us right here and now, is how META-Health has broken down, into specific elements, what a shock is, defining it as a UDIN (an unexpected, dramatic, isolating, no-strategy-to-deal-with event).

What does this mean, and why is it relevant? Well, it helps you to determine what a shock actually is. If we use the example of suddenly losing a loved one, your loss is unexpected, it's dramatic, it makes you feel alone, and you do not know what to do. You have no strategy to deal with what's happened. You freeze. This is a UDIN.

As you are probably not experiencing shaking (which the animals do) as part of your shock release, what can you do to help yourself? Recognition of reactions you may be experiencing as a result of your shock will help. Are you experiencing any of the below?

- Obsessively thinking about what's happened
- Finding it hard to concentrate
- Difficulty sleeping
- Tense muscles
- Loss of appetite
- Cold hands and feet
- Increased adrenaline and cortisol levels (stress hormones).

In the self-help section at the end of the chapter, I have included a muscle relaxation technique which can be extremely beneficial as a gentle starting point to help you deal with a shock. Addressing tension caused by stress can help the body far beyond just the muscles. By regularly practising this exercise, you will not only benefit in the short term, but also reap long-term benefits that will be positive for your whole being.

Among the benefits are:

- A decrease in heart rate
- Lower blood pressure
- A relaxed chest muscle, allowing you to breathe deeper
- Less muscle tension throughout the body, promoting better oxygen levels in the blood
- Brain waves will have moved from beta to alpha, meaning that your mind will feel calmer, with less monkey chatter.

Long-term benefits include:

- Increased ability to cope with stress
- Better sleep
- Better concentration
- Stronger immune system
- Increased energy levels
- Decline in general anxiety and stress
- Improved mood and self-esteem.

You can see that muscle relaxation is well worth doing, as it effectively counteracts the body's reactions to shock.

'An anxious mind cannot exist in a relaxed body.'
Edmund Jacobson

Think of your health and deal with your shock

Unfortunately, the more time passes after a shock which has not been dealt with, the more likely your body will turn it into physical issues to get your attention. Your body will begin by gently saying, 'Please deal with this shock' by making you feel emotionally uncomfortable when you are retriggered by something. If you ignore that persistent alarm call, the message will become more intense, and may possibly show up in the form of a physical problem. That is the body's way of trying harder to get your attention, saying again, *'PLEASE DEAL WITH THIS SHOCK'*, only, as you can see, this time it's speaking louder.

This system is genius, but unfortunately people generally don't get it, and only see physical reactions as symptoms of physical problems. But if you look at the body as a whole, you begin to see that all aspects of it are related. A major emotional shock, as experienced in loss, can ultimately affect our mental and/or our physical health. In my opinion, it is crucial that you look at this aspect of your loss, but the way to do it is slowly and a little at a time. The exercises at the end of this chapter are a continuation of previous exercises, and are designed specifically to deal with any shocks you have experienced. You'll find further tools at appropriate points in the book. Please rest assured that wherever you are on your grieving journey, you can clear any shocks and stuck emotional energy. Considering the enormity of shocks related to loss, they are generally straightforward to deal with. Yes, you did read that correctly.

Let me give you an example of how dealing with your shock can help you, and how it can transform your life.

Claire

Claire was a midwife, and she came to me feeling quite sceptical of what I did. However, she was desperate, and thought that she would just give it a go. She came because she was suffering from intense – almost constant – migraines, and she was finding work very difficult. It wasn't long before she spoke of the stillbirth of her baby two years previous. She was heartbroken. Every day that she went to work, she was helping mothers to have their babies, but she had lost hers. Can you see how every single day she was being retriggered, and that her stuck emotions and the trapped energy of her shock were subsequently manifesting as migraines? Her body was trying to tell her that something was wrong. It was shouting very loudly at her. She hadn't dealt with the shock of her loss or her pain.

We worked together to clear her trapped energy and stuck emotions, with the result that her migraines stopped completely. Yes, *completely*. Her body did not have to continually tell her (via her migraines) that something was wrong anymore, as she had finally dealt with her loss in terms of the shock. I will come back to Claire in chapter 9, where I will develop the connection between emotional issues, which can manifest following a shock, and physical problems.

As this chapter draws to an end, I hope that I have emphasised to you exactly why you need to deal with the shock of loss. My aim has been to introduce you to the whole concept of *shock* and its effects on the body – why you need to deal with it, and the effects of ignoring it. You really do have the power to help yourself out of emotional pain and towards a transformation into joy. Let's be proactive. I invite you to engage in the next two exercises, to gently guide yourself towards identifying and acknowledging any personal shocks that you might have suffered; they are followed by the muscle relaxation exercise mentioned earlier.

Joy Beyond Grief – Self-Love Exercises

Please do these in the order given.

If, having read this chapter, you do not feel that any aspect of your loss involved a shock, please still read through Part 1 - Recognising your Shock (on the next page) to double-check. If after reading them through you still feel the same, that's fine – continue on to the relaxation exercise, as this will still be helpful to you.

I invite you to answer the questions that follow in your journal. By simply answering the questions, you are recognising and acknowledging this part of your grieving process. Writing down your answers gives you additional clarity on this aspect of your loss. And this information will be used in a later chapter in conjunction with some energy techniques.

The aim here is to identify your shock, not to get pulled further into your pain. So please use the heart breathing exercise if you need it. After completing Part 1, move on to Part 2.

Part 1 - Recognising Your Shock

1. Identify your potential shock:

   - Was it when your loved one died suddenly?
   - Was it when your loved one was diagnosed with a terminal illness?
   - Where were you?
   - What were you doing?
   - What time of day was it?
   - What were you wearing?
   - Who were you with?

2. How long ago did the shock aspect of your loss occur?

   - Was it less than or more than a year?

3. Are you aware of any retriggers?

4. What is your emotional state? Have another look at your *Grieving Hearts*. Are you aware that some of the emotions you are feeling are ones that you had experienced quite a lot before your loss? Are there some old familiar feelings?

5. Have you been struggling with any physical issues since your loss?

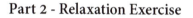

Part 2 - Relaxation Exercise

I invite you to participate in a gentle muscle relaxation exercise, which you should try and incorporate into your daily life. Why? Because if you regularly focus on your muscles relaxing and tensing, as demonstrated in this exercise, it will help both your mind and your body to deal with your loss in a slow and gentle way. It allows the body to gently focus on feeling tense and relaxed. This will be an immense help to you, particularly if done regularly. The benefits of this exercise are numerous and long-term with regular practice.

To listen to this relaxation exercise, please go to my website: www. janicethompson.co.uk. (A transcript of the exercise is provided after the hints.)

Some helpful hints for this relaxation exercise:

1. Make sure you put enough time aside to complete the whole exercise (15 mins).
2. Make sure that you will not be disturbed. Turn off your phone and put a *Do not disturb* sign on the door if necessary.
3. Ensure that you are comfortable. For this exercise, it is best to lie down and have a blanket close by, as you may get cold after lying still for a while.

4. Be aware that as you follow the exercise, your mind will want to wander. But all you need to do is gently bring your awareness back to following the exercise. Focus on each muscle group being worked on.

5. Just allow your feelings to flow – don't force anything.

6. This is an opportunity for your grief buddy to help you. While you're completing the exercise, they could look after your children, help keep others out of the way, or they could read the instructions out to you.

The Muscle Relaxation Exercise

1/ Tense your feet, point your toes downwards, tighten for a few seconds, and then relax them.

2/ Point your toes upwards and tense them. Hold that tension for a few seconds and then relax.

3/ Tighten your thigh muscles (between your knees and hips), hold, and then relax them. Let them go loose.

4/ Tighten your buttocks by squeezing them together tightly. Tense your hip muscles at the front of your body, too. Hold, and then relax, releasing all muscles in this area and letting them sink into the floor.

5/ Tighten the muscles in your back by gently arching it (please be careful if you have a back problem, or miss this one out completely if necessary). Hold, and then completely relax your back into the floor.

6/ Pull in your stomach muscles. Hold and then relax them.

7/ Tighten your chest muscle by taking a deep breath in. Hold, and then release and exhale. Allow all the tension in this area to go.

8/ Tense your shoulder blades by squeezing them in together. Hold, and then relax.

9/ Be aware that all the muscles you have tensed and relaxed are now heavy into the floor.

10/ Tense your shoulders by lifting them up towards your ears. Squeeze them up, and then hold and relax.

11/ Tighten the muscles in the top back of your arms (triceps) by straightening them. Hold, and then relax.

12/ Tighten the muscles in the top front side of your arms (biceps) – best done by imitating a muscle man pose. Tighten and then relax.

13/ Clench your fists tight. Hold and then relax completely.

14/ Moving to your face, tighten your jaw by opening it wide. Hold and then relax it. Let your jaw hang loosely, slightly open.

15/ Squeeze your eyes closed tightly. Squeeze your cheeks by doing a huge smile, and then just relax the muscle.

16/ Tighten the muscles in your forehead by raising your eyebrows as high as you can. Hold, and then relax. Feel a gentle wave of relaxation all across your face and neck. Allow your head to weigh heavy into the floor.

17/ Be aware of your entire body. Is there anywhere still tense? If there is, go back to that muscle group and repeat the tense and relax exercise.

18/ Now allow a blissful wave of relaxation to flow down from your head all the way down to your toes. Visualise this wave as a colour, and see it move gently down your body.

19/ Spend a moment just enjoying this gentle wave of relaxation.

20/ Take a few deep breaths to finish. Get up very slowly, have a drink of water, and carry on with your day.

Please practise this exercise regularly, and take a moment to remember all of these benefits:

- A decreased heart rate
- lower blood pressure
- more relaxed chest muscle, you breathe more deeply
- less muscle tension throughout the body
- better oxygen levels in the blood
- brain waves will have moved from beta to alpha, meaning your mind will feel calmer with less monkey chatter
- improved ability to cope with stress
- better sleep; better concentration
- stronger immune system
- increased energy levels
- decline in general anxiety and stress levels
- improved mood and self-esteem

Note: This exercise is suitable for children.

Chapter 4

PAIN, SUFFERING, AND LETTING GO

'Pain is inevitable, suffering is optional.'
Old Zen Proverb

I CAME ACROSS THIS ZEN proverb early in my grief work. It's a very powerful and meaningful statement on many levels, and is so helpful in understanding grief and loss. I am going to spend some time breaking down its meaning to help you understand the difference between pain and suffering, and also help you to explore where you are. Let's start with 'Pain is inevitable'.

Pain is inevitable

We can experience different types of pain: physical pain, emotional pain, and even mental pain. Pain can be experienced with varying degrees of intensity, from mild to extreme, and what causes us pain can vary greatly from person to person. However, every person who has ever walked the Earth will have experienced some kind of pain at some point in his or her life. Pain is universal and a fundamental part of Nature. Everything in the natural world has meaning, so what is the meaning of pain? Specifically, what is the meaning of the intense pain felt in grief?

Pain basically and clearly tells you that something is wrong. This is obvious when we look at losing a loved one. It is clear what is wrong – the person we love so deeply has gone, at least in the physical sense (see chapter 8 for a further discussion on this). Our depth of pain is a barometer for us to make sense of our world. For example, if someone we hardly know dies, we feel sad, but this is a mild pain compared to when someone very close to us passes. The closer we are to something or someone, the more it means to us if we lose them. Again, this is obvious. It is what we do about the pain that matters. The pain is unavoidable if we have loved, but how best can we help ourselves through it? At the end of this chapter, there are some more self-help exercises, but to be honest, every exercise in the book is designed to help you deal with that pain.

Pain gives meaning to our loss. The connection we had with our loved ones would have little significance to us if we didn't feel the pain of loss. The more intense the pain, the more you have loved. Gurus, philosophers, academics, and healers throughout the centuries have discussed and written about the true nature of pain. Although they often view it from wildly differing perspectives, there is often the recurring idea that pain carries the potential to help someone grow and expand.

> 'You will not grow if you sit in a beautiful flower
> garden, but you will grow if you are sick, if you are
> in pain, if you experience losses, and if you do not
> put your head in the sand, but take the pain as a
> gift to you with a very, very specific purpose.'
> Elizabeth Kübler-Ross

The thought of that intense feeling holding any potential at all may seem absurd at the moment, but be assured there are those who have travelled a similar journey to yours; they have experienced this potential in the form of growth and expansion into a place of joy, and this includes myself and many of my clients.

But for now, I invite you to just be open about this and acknowledge where you are and acknowledge your pain. Let's work towards easing it as much as possible.

Suffering is optional

Having gained a better understanding of pain, let us now turn our attention to the second part of the proverb: 'Suffering is optional.' What is suffering? How is it different from pain? How do we avoid it? Can we avoid it? And what on earth is meant by *optional*? Suffering *is* optional – no, really!

Let's answer one at a time. Suffering occurs when pain is not addressed. Prolonged pain turns into suffering, and is actually the result of pain not being dealt with. Suffering can certainly be avoided by first acknowledging your pain, getting a little more specific about it, and then helping yourself through it.

Deirdre

Let me give you an example of what I mean. At the age of seven, Deirdre lost her baby brother, who was three at the time. He had wandered off from the house and drowned. This was certainly extremely painful for Deirdre, but additionally, her mother had blamed her for his death. Deirdre came to me at the age of fifty-eight. She had been suffering with the pain of the loss of her baby brother for over fifty years, and throughout those years her beliefs about herself, her guilt, and pain had consumed her. Would things have been different if, at the time of his death, she had been able to mourn his loss or had received support through her pain, as well as reassurance that it wasn't her fault? Of course, we shall never know for sure, but I strongly believe that her life would have been a bit easier. Having said that, she did finally seek help: we worked together on all her feelings related to her loss and her life is very different today.

Unfortunately, like Deirdre, there are many people still suffering with the same painful feelings years after a loss. Even when they appear to stem from different causes, these feelings often refer back to an unresolved loss, and that's how life patterns occur (I go into this more deeply in chapter 9). So often, people do not seem to be aware of where their pain has come from because so many years have passed. There is often confusion because they don't believe that their loss can still be affecting them.

I am sure that you have heard people saying, 'She never got over the loss of …', or 'He's not been the same since …', or 'He has become so bitter because of …'. Sadly, I have encountered many clients in this situation. What makes this even sadder is that many of them just didn't realise that things could be different. Does this resonate with you? If so, please know things can be different for you even if, like Deirdre, a long period of time has passed. The techniques explained later in this book can help you shift out of struggle and into peace.

To clarify, deal with your pain and avoid continual suffering, which can become so engrained that you actually believe that is who you are. Deirdre at fifty-eight believed that she was her true self, but without the effects of that continual suffering, who might she truly have been and what might she have done differently, all those years? Luckily, as we worked together, under those layers of struggle she found her beautiful soul that she could have compassion for, and her life became very much better for it.

A *suffering* you is not a *true* you. It is not who you are – not truly. It is simply undealt-with pain manifesting as anger, bitterness, jealousy, or any other number of uncomfortable feelings. They *seem* to be a part of you, but that is an illusion. Additionally, left unchecked, continual suffering can develop into physical issues. This has already been touched upon in the previous chapter, and will be discussed further in chapter 9.

Regarding 'suffering is optional': what is meant by that is that ultimately if you are still suffering many years after a loss, although not strictly optional, you do not need to still be suffering; rather, you have the option to change – to alleviate that ongoing suffering.

Let's keep moving along on our journey together, having now got to grips with why you need to acknowledge and address your pain and avoid perpetuating it. If you feel you have been suffering for a long period of time with a loss, or if you have now come to realise that a previous loss has been affecting you, my friend, please keep reading this book. It has been written to help you.

From a medical viewpoint, any ongoing suffering could be labelled as 'complicated grief', more recently known as 'persistent complex bereavement disorder' in the *Diagnostic and Statistical Manual of Mental Disorders, 5th ed. (DSM-5)*. This is a manual the medical profession uses to diagnose mental illnesses. The *International Classification of Disease (ICD-11)*, which is recognised by the World Health Organisation (WHO), would call it 'prolonged grief disorder'.

Although I have significant personal issues with calling any form of grieving a 'disorder', it is reassuring that there is some form of recognition for those experiencing ongoing suffering. If you have been diagnosed with any of the above, keep reading with the knowledge that you can come out of this. You are experiencing a natural reaction to an unresolved grief or related issue. By recognising this, you have given yourself the power to change things. You have the potential to learn something about yourself and change your life – actually, to *transform* it. For more information on the different types of grief that have been recognised, please go to my website: www.janicethompson.co.uk

Whether you are in the early days of loss, experiencing that acute pain, or if you have been suffering for some time without knowing that the suffering was about a loss, understanding the difference between pain and suffering is key. The pain of loss is inevitable, but if you deal with it directly, you are choosing to say *No* to continual suffering. For that alone, you deserve a massive pat on the back. One thing that can be a huge hindrance to ending any form of suffering is the inability to *let go*, so let's take a closer look at this.

Letting go

What does letting go actually mean? I'll begin with a few very important points. Letting go is about awareness. It is not about me suggesting to you that you have to let go of everything – or anything come to that – that can be fear-provoking: this is not what this is about. It is about understanding the concept, as it is a very misunderstood aspect of loss. For you, it may be easier to simply focus on inviting love in, as opposed to letting go of the pain. Taking any action around letting go is a very personal issue, so be aware of what resonates best with you. Also, differentiating between letting go emotionally and letting go of physical items can be enlightening, and both will be addressed here.

Letting go emotionally

In my work, I have often heard comments about letting go when someone has lost a loved one. For example, 'I just can't let him/her go.' … 'How can I let go of someone I have been with all my life?' … 'How can I let go, when we were so close?' … 'I don't know how to let go.' … These four comments, and others like them, are extremely commonplace, and I am sure that you have heard something similar, or perhaps you have said something similar about your own loss. If you take these comments literally, they don't make much sense. Your loved one has passed away, so you can't lose them any more than you already have. However, there is a very real sense that if you let go of *something,* you are going to lose the loved one forever in some way. What is that *something*?

More often than not, that something is related to the pain. If you let go of the pain, you believe you will end up further away from your loved one. By hanging onto the pain in some way, not necessarily on a conscious level, you believe that you can remain close to them. You may feel that you can't let go because you feel guilty about something, and therefore deserve to keep suffering. You worry that if you let go of the pain and feel OK, you will forget your loved one. Some people feel that letting go of these feelings is tantamount to disrespecting their loved one. However, this could not be further from the truth.

Generally, feelings surrounding a death are painful ones. These emotions are showing you just how much you loved the deceased, but by holding onto sadness, guilt, misery, etc., you are quite literally blocking your body's systems on all levels. This is usually not a conscious decision, and occurs as part of the freeze response discussed previously.

These emotions literally freeze and get stuck with us. They get stuck in our body's systems, particularly our energy system. If left unattended, they can become a source of continual suffering, either consciously, through knowing that they came from your loss, or subconsciously, by experiencing them regularly without knowing where they stem from. You come to believe that is who you are, but no, my friend, that is not who you are. It is merely who you *think* you are. These are only feelings – you are far more magnificent, beautiful, and loving than that. There is far more to you than just your feelings. When it feels right in your heart, that is the time to take action around letting go. If ultimately letting go of pain is a good move, and the opposite of letting go is *holding on*, what exactly would feel good to hold onto? The answer is *love*. Recall the memories of wonderful times passed – not analysing them, but simply allowing yourself to enjoy those comforting, loving feelings that you have for your loved one. This can be very difficult to do when you are filled with pain, but releasing that pain allows you to emotionally tune back into those times you had together, which were special to the extent of being timeless. Nothing and no one can take those memories away from you. Often, what happens is that we confuse our feelings of love with the pain that we experienced, and then we hold onto the pain, thinking that is how we show love. Showing love is letting that pain go, and becoming reconnected with the true love held between you.

> 'Grief can be the garden of compassion. If you
> keep your heart open through everything,
> your pain can become your greatest ally in
> your life's search for love and wisdom.'
> Rumi

When you allow space for love and are able, if only for a short while initially, to focus on those loving memories and feelings, something magical happens. This love allows for a new, closer connection to your loved ones from a more spiritual perspective. I cannot tell you how many times I have witnessed this with a client, as they have moved from feeling the pain to feeling their loved one around them, to smelling their loved one's natural smell, or developing an inner knowing of what their loved one thought about particular ideas, to seeing signs that indicate their loved one is near.

For myself, it has always been about buzzards. Yes, that's right, I said buzzards. They keep coming into my life, often in some very interesting ways. Why buzzards? My husband used to keep them. This wonderful connection definitely went up a notch when I let go of a lot of pain around the loss of my husband. I had crazy things happen, like seeing five buzzards in a row on a telegraph pole after I had asked Andy to be near to me, and on one occasion, a buzzard actually crashed into my kitchen window. Believe me, my kitchen window is difficult to crash into, especially for a bird of that size. The bird was fine, though. He just shook himself off and flew away.

I see now, that initially, I just couldn't *let go* because I did not have a conscious awareness that I was holding onto my sadness. I just had this overwhelming fear of letting go and I didn't want to do it. It was a very scary feeling, as though I was standing on the precipice of a void. However, when I understood what letting go meant, I realised it wasn't a void at all – it was a peaceful, reflective space for me. And, fascinatingly, when I understood that, well, that's when the *buzzard* magic began for me.

I cannot say how you will feel closer to your loved one – we are all different – but therein lies the beauty of this. Be open, listen, smell, and look around, because often messages are out there, but we just don't see them. Simply allow yourself to be open to the idea that letting go of pain can allow the love that is – and always will be – there to flow. You are not letting go of your loved one: you are simply making more room for your love's connection to shine through. In fact, you may even experience a new sense of closeness to the one you have lost.

Letting go physically

What do you keep? What do you let go of? This is such an individual choice, and maybe not something that you even want to be thinking about at this moment in time. Perhaps read this for future reference, and then come back to it again when you are ready.

I initially kept everything when my husband died, and I mean everything, from old pants to his wallet, to his old work boots and even his toothbrush. Gradually, I did get rid of some things, and what I realise now, and would like to share with you, is this: I had even kept the sweatshirt (which was his) that I was wearing the evening he died, and which had some blood on it from where he had fallen and hurt his nose. I kept it because I felt it brought me closer to him somehow. But really, holding on to this sweatshirt was not helping me in any way, and it constantly reminded me of that fateful day. It didn't remind me of the love between Andy and myself, and it didn't bring any relief to my heart. It only kept me focusing on the pain. I let the sweatshirt go, and now I have a select few items that remind me of our love together. I am telling you this to help you think about what you may or may not want to keep. I invite you to consider keeping those things that remind you of the love and not the pain – to keep those cherished, love-filled items, and not things which remind you of your loved one's passing or any other painful memories.

A flavour of things to come

Having read this chapter, at some point in your grieving process it will feel right to work towards letting the pain go, as you learn to bring in love and avoid ongoing suffering. Simply being aware of this will help the process. You will know what helps to keep hold of emotionally, such as love feelings, and what to hold onto physically, in terms of selecting a few special items. All of this, my fellow traveller, is massive – a truly remarkable demonstration of the human spirit. The rest of the book deals with helping you with tools that you can use when you are ready. You are a remarkable being, and I would like to honour that. May I politely remind you that this is not a book about *getting over* your loss. It is a book of positive transformation that can occur *because* of your loss. One small step at a time (or a large step, if you prefer).

Letting go of the pain often releases enormous energy which can have the potential to transform your life. We want to use the enormous energy found within grief to transform your life. Obviously, not in some fast, shallow way, but in a true, deep, meaningful way, which incorporates honouring the one you have lost.

Brenda

Brenda came to me regarding her grief following the loss of her granddaughter. She was very distraught, and over the course of a few sessions, it became apparent that she was in a place of suffering where her pain of loss was as strong as the day that she first experienced it, which had been a few years prior. It was causing problems to herself and in her marriage. If anything, it seemed to be growing in intensity. She had stopped all social activities and never did anything without her husband.

We worked on several issues, many of which stemmed from her younger years and which initially seemed unrelated, save for some common triggers. However, after a few sessions, she saw a connection between the loss of her granddaughter and those earlier issues which were connected by feelings of guilt: she saw how she had behaved in her youth became interlinked with guilt about not being able to save her granddaughter from death. As we cleared this stuck pain (remember how a previous shock can affect a subsequent one), Brenda came to understand how this connection had become intermingled with her loss and by understanding it, she was able to move forward. She began to go out more with her friends, which eased the pressure on her marriage and allowed her to experience the things in life that she enjoyed. She didn't just get to a point of coping – she went way past that and transformed her life into a much more fulfilling one. Incidentally, she told me she felt a much closer connection to her deceased granddaughter because of it.

Be open, fellow traveller, to pushing past points that you cannot even comprehend at the moment, not forgetting that just because you can't grasp them now, that doesn't mean they're not there. Remember also that transformation can come in many forms. For Brenda, it was in the form of more freedom to feel safe and confident in doing things on her own. For some, it could be a career change, while others experience a change in beliefs on spirituality. Be open, and consider what your change could be.

Joy Beyond Grief – Self-Love Exercises

Please answer the following questions. You may wish to make a note of them in your journal, and have your grief buddy with you to support you through them. Please remember to be responsible for your wellbeing here, and if at any time you feel overwhelmed with emotions, STOP! Do your heart breathing, get up, move around, and do something different until you feel ready to come back to them.

1/ Has your loss come in the past 12 months, or was it over 12 months ago?

2/ In light of our distinction between pain and suffering, do you consider yourself to be experiencing raw pain, or do you feel that you have been suffering for an extended period of time?

3/ Do you feel guilty about anything you did or didn't do regarding your loss?

4/ Do you believe that you are in any way responsible for the loss of your loved one?

5/ If many years have passed since your loss, do you still get very emotionally upset when you think about them, or always rerun a particularly painful aspect of your loss?

6/ If some time has passed since your loss, do you get overly emotional at funerals?

7/ Do you feel as though you just can't let go of your loved one?

8/ Do you find it hard to think of the good memories?

9/ Have you kept many clothes, possessions, and other items related to the one you have lost – that are not from a memory of love – and you just can't let go of them?

10/ Do you feel you are being disrespectful if you don't always feel upset when you think about the one you have lost?

These questions are designed to help you understand whether you are in the natural process of feeling pain after a recent loss, or if you are *suffering* (which is obviously natural in terms of what happens if pain is left undealt with, but is unnecessary) as the result of prolonged pain. They will help you to see whether or not you are hanging on to some negative aspects of your loss. Either way, it's OK. It's all about awareness of where you are.

Here is the next exercise for you. I strongly recommend that you complete it with your grief buddy present.

Grounding yourself

Sit comfortably and take your awareness to your heart area. Do a couple of your heart breaths, and then allow your awareness to move down towards your feet. Imagine your feet sprouting roots that extend far into the ground, just like a tree. Let them anchor you to the Earth – strong, powerful roots holding you solid. Now move on to the next part of the exercise.

From your *Healing Heart* I invite you to choose a feeling and its intensity that is near to the 0 in the centre of the heart. Perhaps choose one that you feel you may be able to let go of, even if only a little. Please do not deal with any feelings towards the outside of the heart, as those are too intense. We will address those later in the book. Alternatively, you can use an emotion that you are feeling at this moment – if it's not too intense.

Allow yourself to be with that feeling. Don't judge it. Don't try to resist it. Don't analyse or try to push it away. Simply allow it to be.

I now invite you to be fully present with that feeling, and simply answer the following questions. Do not think about them too much – just a quick, straightforward answer is all that's needed. There is no right or wrong. This is simply about awareness.

1/ At this moment in time, am I able to let this feeling go?

2/ Is it OK for this feeling to be here?

3/ How does this feeling serve me?

4/ Am I willing to consider letting it go?

Simply see what these questions bring up. For now, just make a note in your journal of what came up. This is still the awareness stage. However, please remember that, sometimes, awareness alone is enough to shift things. Don't fight the feeling, or any of the answers to the questions. These questions could also be used for letting go of any physical items (simply replace the word *feeling* with any physical item you wish).

If it is very obvious that you can let something go at this stage, you could try one of many letting-go rituals, such as writing something down on a piece of paper, and then burning the paper with a clear intention of letting it go. You could imagine putting the feeling into a small container and burying it in the ground, where it disintegrates into nothing, or you could blow it out into the universe, where it dissolves. Whatever feels right for you. If, however, letting go seems too difficult at this moment in time, that's fine. In chapter 6, I will give you a powerful tool to help with this, if and when it feels right for you to use it.

Now, simply invite some love and peace in, in any form you choose. Allowing a nurturing feeling into your heart, think of something beautiful in nature, or a picture you love – something that means love and peace to you. Simply stay with this for a few moments, and I will see you in the next chapter.

Chapter 5

EVERYTHING IS ENERGY

'I cannot believe such monstrous energy
of grief can lead to nothing.'
John Gardner

I WAS STUCK TO THE seat, my heart was pounding, but I wasn't afraid. In fact, I was remarkably calm and accepting of what was happening to me ... whatever *it* was. It was certainly all a little strange. Actually, it was very strange. I had an overwhelming sense that my body was realigning, readjusting. My whole body felt very tingly and my ankles began to swell quite considerably, so much so that the people sitting near me were noticing.

Suddenly, I had an urge to go to the toilet. A couple of colleagues offered to help me, as I could barely stand up, which, for a fit thirty-seven-year-old, was rather comical. I say comical, because I must have looked so funny hobbling along, propped up by my colleagues, very unsure of my footing. It seemed so surreal, as if I was starring in my own crazy movie. I managed to reach the toilet, and gradually the symptoms subsided. I was fine, if a little exhausted. So, what was that all about?

More about META-Health

I was in Bristol, on a ten-day META-Health course, which also incorporated learning a new therapy – Advanced Clearing Energetics (ACE), developed by Richard Flook. I had been interested in META-Health since hearing about it a few months earlier, and little did I know when I signed up for this course what a huge impact it would have on my healing journey.

META-Health, as I mentioned earlier, is a way of looking at illness and disease from a totally new perspective. It focuses on what causes an illness, what is behind the symptoms, and basically what caused the problem in the first place. With many medical professionals readily admitting that they do not know what causes up to 95 per cent of illnesses, the general consensus is that stress can either be the root cause of illness, or can exacerbate the problem. With that in mind, I decided to sign up for this course and consider the new ideas that it proposed. With my own stress levels being extremely high at the time, I thought I might gain some insight into how much this stress was affecting my body.

I had managed to get myself into a very destructive relationship after my husband died. This was not something I had ever experienced before, and at the time I had no idea whatsoever as to why I was allowing such a person into my life. However, one thing was for sure: I couldn't seem to get quit of him. The relationship was also affecting my daughters, causing them a lot of pain and upset, and yet every time I tried to end it, I couldn't. I was hurting, and became extremely angry with myself. Being incapable of ending something that I knew was not good for me had me feeling helpless and hopeless, but by the time the course in Bristol had finished, it was all totally clear to me why I hadn't walked away from what I knew in my heart was a toxic relationship. It all made perfect sense.

On this particular day, I'd begun discussing some small health issue and I ended up talking about my relationship. I was working with a couple of other participants on the course and as part of the process, they were using an energy technique with me. I soon began to get very emotional, which drew Richard's attention. He asked me a couple of questions about what I was gaining from being in this destructive relationship, and then suddenly the penny dropped. *I was gaining being miserable!!* Yes, that is what I said, *I was gaining being miserable.* I was so, so sad about losing my husband that, subconsciously, I didn't want to be happy.

So, what better way to stay unhappy than to be with someone who made me really unhappy? Brilliant! But, very upsetting and very painful. This was a total revelation. It was something I had not been consciously aware of, but during this course I was able to access my subconscious mind via the use of ACE, which brought these issues into my conscious awareness, and there I was able to deal with them.

There was a change in me, demonstrated visibly by that trip to the toilet, and I felt very different – so much so that I just knew that I could end the relationship. It was a deep inner knowing, a gentle and quiet voice. I knew 100 per cent that it was over, and I knew I would be able to go back and tell him. It was highly significant that my fellow participants were using an energy technique on me at the time of my realisation, because prior to that I had talked the hind legs off every donkey that would listen to me about my unhappy relationship. However, I had never had that realisation before. What had happened? What was different that time? The technique allowed me to tap into my own body's energy system – THAT was the difference. I shall come back to this story later on in the chapter.

The reason why I am sharing this part of my journey with you is to show you the sheer power of your own body's energy system. It can shift and change your physical body as well as your psychological and mental self. I use the term *self* to represent various different aspects of us. This chapter will explore all that is energy, frequency, and vibration in preparation for the following chapter. Human energy could fill a book all by itself, so I am going to keep this quite brief, but if you are interested, further readings will be in the *Resources* section at the back of the book.

We will begin by looking at the bigger picture of energy. As quantum physics tells us, everything is energy – and it doesn't get much bigger than that. We will look at your body as a gathering of energy, addressing its specific energy system, and learning what vibration and frequency mean to your body. This will all provide a basis for delving into the topic of connectedness, and some specific aspects of energy and grief.

Everything is energy

Quantum physics has been studied for many years but unfortunately has not been widely taught in schools or recognised in the wider community. This I feel is detrimental because without an understanding of how quantum physics affects the world and more specifically you and me, it can be difficult to help ourselves in everyday life. This includes helping ourselves through a grieving experience. We have only been taught a Newtonian way of understanding the world, i.e. that everything is solid; however, quantum physics shows that everything is actually energy.

> 'The day science begins to study non-physical
> phenomena, it will make more progress in one decade
> than in all the previous centuries of its existence.'
> Nikola Tesla

Everything is made of energy? Yes, that is right: everything. From the chair you're sitting on to the pages of this book you are reading – all matter is comprised of energy. Absolutely everything in our universe is made up of energy. I know it can be hard to believe, but think about electricity. It isn't difficult to understand that electricity is energy; whereas if I say the same of a solid bookshelf or a human being, it quickly becomes more challenging to accept. It's all energy, though! Some things appear just too solid to be energy, but if you continue down in size, beyond the atomic level, you get to pure energy. This energy is vibrational in nature.

This is where it all starts to get interesting. Everything is vibrating. I am vibrating and you are vibrating. I know you don't feel like you are vibrating right now, but I can assure you, you are. It's just so subtle that you can't feel it. You don't feel the Earth spinning, and that's despite it doing a full rotation every day – pretty fast. Yes, we are vibrating – all of us are energy beings. *WOW!!!* And there you were, thinking that you were solid!

You appear solid because the energy particles in your body are packed so tightly that they create a form, a physical shape. Compare this to the wind, where the energy particles are loosely packed, creating a light, non-visual movement of air. Generally, we are vibrating very slowly, making us appear solid. The more solid the thing, the more slowly it vibrates, thus appearing more solid. The more fluid the thing, the faster it vibrates. You are a vibrating wave of energy, and you have your own personal energy frequency.

Your vibration

Every part of you is in a state of vibration. Each system in your body – every organ, bone, and tissue – is vibrating, and they all have their own optimal frequency of vibration. When we are in a state of good health – mentally, physically, and psychologically – all those frequencies come together in a harmonious state. However, when some frequency that is counter to your health comes into some part of your body, it causes disharmony, and that is what we know as disease.

What causes the frequency to go into disharmony? There are several things that can affect vibrational states, including your inner thoughts, your feelings, your beliefs, your environment, and events in your life. Remember when we discussed how our energy is seriously disrupted when we experience a shock, such as the death of a loved one? Well, that energy disruption will almost certainly affect your vibrational state. Left undealt with, this has the potential to affect your whole body, and can go on to cause physical problems and/or continual suffering. This disruption – this altered vibrational state, moving away from its natural frequency – can be brought back into harmony through various means, including using techniques that are specifically aimed at working on this energy system.

We are working towards raising your vibration, as the higher the vibration you experience, the better you will feel. This is not only relevant to grief, but in all areas of life. The more we clear in terms of trauma, shock or anything that throws us off balance, the more we can experience being in a high vibration. The good news is that there are some relatively simple things you can do to raise your vibration. Even something as easy as allowing yourself to have a good cry can raise your vibration. It's nature's way of helping to balance the sadness, and can be seen as self-compassionate.

Self-compassion, kindness, and ultimately love – all raise our vibration. Heart breathing will help raise your vibration too.

Your energy system

Having established that you are made of pure energy, we now turn our attention to the specific system within your body that energy flows through – the meridian system. Unfortunately, much like our emotions and feelings, this system is so often overlooked by most of society. It is not studied in schools, doctors do not mention it, it is never talked about at work, it is not spoken of in hospitals, and it's rarely discussed in counselling sessions. Yet researchers have known about it for a long time, and certain cultures have taken it very seriously for many thousands of years – well before modern medicine came into being. Modern medicine does not recognise this system, as it goes against its rigid and mechanical ways of viewing the body. Conversely, in China, as well as in various other Eastern cultures, understanding the body's energy system (the meridian system) is a fundamental part of their approach to medicine. They use it to help heal the body of physical, psychological, and emotional problems.

Our energy system is not something that you can see on an x-ray, nor can it be dissected in a lab. You cannot see it, but you can discern the effects of it. The meridian system works in conjunction with the systems of the body that you can see, such as the digestive and circulatory systems. In Chinese medicine, it is all about energy, and the belief that this is at the heart of keeping all systems running in a positive state of balance and vibrational harmony. Whatever is going on with you emotionally, physically, or mentally will affect your energy system.

Every experience you have in life will have an effect on your energy system. If something awful happens, like losing a loved one, this will have a major impact on your energy system. Imagine how it must look when arteries clog up with cholesterol and the blood doesn't flow properly. That's what happens to your energy flow – it gets clogged up. Conversely, if you experience something that makes you feel wonderful – something that makes your heart sing – this will have a positive effect on your energy system, allowing it to flow freely. Basically, if you feel good, your energy is flowing well, and if you feel bad, your energy is disrupted. Your emotions are like a barometer of how well your energy system is flowing.

Your meridians

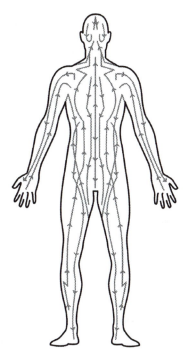

MERIDIAN LINES

Your meridians can be thought of as an interconnecting web of energy lines, running throughout the body. This energy is also known as chi or Qi. Each meridian line is related to the function of a specific organ in the body, but that doesn't mean that its role is limited to servicing a particular organ in isolation, as each organ is also related to a specific emotional experience which will have an impact on this system. These meridians are delicate, quite elusive, and have points along the lines known as acupoints. When stimulated, they can have an effect on the correlating internal organ and can help promote a healthy flow of energy. This is known as the vital breath.

There are also chakra points, which are specific points along the front and the back of the body. There are seven major chakras on the body itself, and several located below and above the body. They are like small vortexes of energy, and many alternative therapies recognise these chakras as playing a vital role in maintaining our overall health.

CHAKRA POINTS

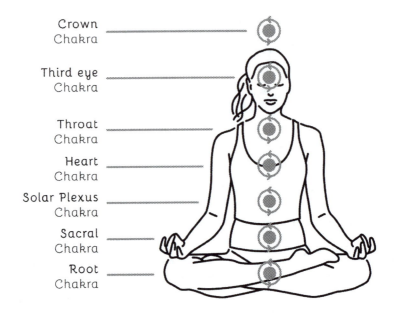

Crown
Chakra

Third eye
Chakra

Throat
Chakra

Heart
Chakra

Solar Plexus
Chakra

Sacral
Chakra

Root
Chakra

Your energy system and grief

And now, I'll bring together all that I have discussed in this chapter, to explain exactly how grief can affect your energy system and vibration. The pain and sadness of your loss will be affecting you as a whole, including all of your body's systems, and especially your energy system. The shock of your loss will have definitely disrupted this system, and all aspects of your loss will add to the disruption. The pain of your loss and all of the perceived negative emotions associated with it along with upsetting memories will be affecting your energy system. This is inevitable, and left unresolved it could have the potential to develop into various health problems. It's a continuation of suffering, as discussed in the previous chapter. However, using strategies and techniques described in the next few chapters, you can help yourself to rebalance and calm this disruption. If you are mindful of this energy system, and look after it, you are taking a massive, positive step towards helping yourself at this difficult time.

Let us return to my story now. So, how was I able to end my unhappy relationship, and how was this related to my energy system? Well, as you will recall, my colleagues were using an energy technique, and this technique had a positive effect on various acupoints of my meridian system. As they were putting the technique into practice, they were, in effect, clearing the blockages in my body's energy flow; they were dealing with the disruption in my energy system caused by my grief. My unhappiness was the result of my loss, which in turn had led me into a destructive relationship, keeping me unhappy. By clearing the blockage, my body then realigned my energy flow, and although I experienced some quite extraordinary physical symptoms, they only lasted a short while before I began to feel so much better. Some people do not feel any physical symptoms at all during this process.

It was my realisation, brought up from my subconscious mind into my conscious awareness as a result of this energy technique, which sparked the reaction. This is the real beauty of it all. It brings forth information buried deep in your subconscious, and delivers it to your conscious awareness where you can deal with it. I was experiencing intense emotions, and my energy flow was affected; however, it had not yet got to a point where my physical health was suffering. For me, it was about the emotional pain, not any physical pain. That might have come later if I hadn't dealt with it when I did.

I have worked with many clients whose grief, unfortunately, had manifested into physical problems. We are very resilient creatures, and it takes a lot of screaming from our bodies, trying to tell us that something is wrong, before the message becomes physical. Are you listening to your body? Following the exercises in this book will help you to listen to your body, clear any energy blockages, and help you to feel better – gently and with self-compassion.

We are all connected

In Chinese medicine, it is believed that Qi (the vital energy) that flows through our bodies gives us life, and also connects us to the universe.

How does this work? What does Chinese medicine mean by 'We are all connected'?

For centuries, the ancients perpetuated the idea that we are all connected, and many other cultures, religions, spiritual leaders, and gurus have since spoken of this universal link. Happily, it appears as though science is finally catching up.

David Bohm has been described as one of the most significant theoretical physicists of the twentieth century. He was highly regarded as a quantum physicist, too. He suggested that 'at the subatomic level, all points in space are essentially the same.'[1] This is also known as non-locality, which states everything is interconnected, i.e. there are no separate parts: everything is connected to everything else. He also went on to explain that any information could be transferred instantly.

That certainly can take a bit of brainpower to get your head around! Let's deal gently with one point at a time, starting with *we are all connected*. The concept that an invisible network of energy connects everyone and everything is widely accepted now. However, those working in the field have called this by different names. For example, Lynne McTaggart[2] calls it *'the Field'*, Karl Dawson[3] calls it *'the Matrix'*, David Wilcock[4] calls it *'the Source Field'*, and Rupert Sheldrake[5] calls it *'the morphogenetic field'*. Whatever the name, they all appear to be referring to the same source of connection between everyone and everything. For so long, we were led to believe that the space between things was empty, but the amount of scientific evidence against this theory is now overwhelming. That so-called empty space is actually a massive web of energetic connection.

Let's look at a connection that you might already be aware of – that of close relatives and even close friends. Have you ever thought about someone, and then they've called you? What about when you're thinking something, and your partner says it? Have you ever felt as though someone needed you, and then when you've called him or her, you've found that they were upset about something? These have been called coincidences, but there are just too many of them for that explanation to hold water. "Synchronicities" is a much better term. Can you think of any other examples of something like this happening?

Heart and Earth connection

One theory is that our connections to each other, and our connections to the Earth are similar and interconnected in two ways. Firstly, humans have meridian lines running through them and the Earth has ley lines running through it. Secondly, the human body has an electromagnetic field radiating from the heart and the Earth has an electromagnetic field radiating from its interior too. Both people's and the Earth's electromagnetic fields are interconnected and information is transferred between them all the time. The diagram below shows exactly how the heart's and the Earth's magnetic fields run the same way, in the beautiful doughnut shape known as a torus.

THE ELECTROMAGNETIC FIELD OF THE HEART

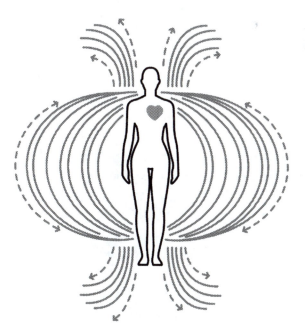

THE ELECTROMAGNETIC FIELD
OF THE EARTH

Very early on, I talked about HeartMath, that amazing organisation based in America, which has been studying the power of the heart and its various connections since the 1970s. Please check out their website in the *Resources* section, as they have done some truly inspiring work. In the meantime, here are a few extremely relevant facts relating to their work:

- The heart's electromagnetic field can be measured up to 8 feet from the body.
- In foetal development, the heart starts to beat even before the brain begins to develop.
- The heart actually has a brain of its own.
- The electromagnetism of the heart is 60 times greater in amplitude than that of the brain.

- When people touch or are near to one another, transference of electromagnetic energy produced by the heart occurs.
- A mother's brainwaves can synchronise with her baby's heartbeat.
- The heart's electromagnetic field contains information and coding which can be influenced by positive or negative emotions.

When people practise heart-focused techniques (including the heart breathing exercise throughout the book), they have an effect on the energy field which makes it easier for others to connect with their hearts. This can lead to creating social coherence, and therefore a happier world for us all to live in. The HeartMath Institute have even developed a Global Coherence Initiative (GCI), which aims 'to unite millions of people worldwide in heart-focused care and intention, to help shift global consciousness from instability and discord to balance, cooperation, and enduring peace'.[6]

Heart connections produce love between lovers, friends, parents and children – and how beautiful those love connections are. As you well know, that is why it's so painful when we lose a loved one. However, when contemplating the ideas that everything is energy and everything is connected, how big of a leap is it then to say that these connections can bridge the life-death divide? Supporting this is Einstein's discovery that energy cannot be created or destroyed; it can only be changed from one form to another. This may be true of life and death.

Connections after death

Could our love connections continue unbroken across the life-death divide? Is there even a real divide at all? A love connection can have some very profound and interesting qualities. To help explain what I mean by this, here is a study which not only clearly shows how loved ones are connected, but also how that connection can traverse space and time.

Studies in quantum physics have shown that couples can maintain some form of connection when in different rooms. In this particular psychological research study, one of the participants was shown a picture depicting different emotional states, while the other was sat alone in a different room. Both of them had their emotional responses measured throughout. What was found was remarkable. Not only did they both respond to the various emotional pictures in the same way, but they did so at *exactly the same time.*[7] Yes, exactly the same time! Not only were they connected in terms of brain responses, they were also doing it simultaneously. Something was connecting them – something invisible to the naked eye. Could it be this energy connection?

Unfortunately, grief can make you feel so disconnected – disconnected from your loved one, from yourself, and even from everyone else around you. I totally appreciate that the love connection you once knew can feel like it has been torn apart, but maybe by looking at the change in nature of your love connection, a new understanding can follow. Remember, neither space nor time affected the connection described in the study. Maybe the veil between you and your loved one is thinner than you think: maybe your loved one is just in another room.

'I have only slipped into the next room,
I am I and you are you.
Whatever we were to each other, that we are still.'
Henry Scott Holland

I have often heard people say that when a loved one has died, *a part of them has died, too.* Maybe that part of them, or indeed that part of you, was actually a frequency of energy. When two people's energy systems are steadfastly entwined, it can truly feel as though part of one has been lost in the passing of the other. It may feel like that from a purely physical perspective, and because of the immense emotions that you are experiencing, but if we allow ourselves to see this from a *no-difference-in-space-and-time* angle, maybe it'll become easier to feel as though the energy between you both has simply jumped frequency, and not gone away forever. What if, no matter how long it has been since your loved one has died, they really are always with you? Always connected. This can allow a door to remain open, through which the new form of love connection between you both can freely pass.

Everyone – and everything – is connected with the ability to tune in to the field of information, and receive that information simultaneously. Looking at the entwined energy between you and your deceased loved one, your emotional bond is that of love, and therefore it can never truly be severed. Please bear this in mind whenever you feel alone. Your loved one may be a lot closer than you realise, so if it feels right, speak to them. Speak from your heart, and start to look out for little signs in return. Such signs may be very subtle or very obvious. Remember the buzzards!

Perhaps you may not immediately see, feel, or hear any signs, and that is OK, too. Be kind to yourself, and when the time is right, things may change. In the meantime, ensure that the connection between you and those supporting you (including your grief buddy) is there in the form of emotional support. You can now see just how connected you (and we all) are, so please make use of that loving energy connection.

Back to my story

As well as loving energy connections, there are obviously connections between those who spend a lot of time together. Such was the connection between myself and the person I became involved with after my husband's death. I believe the shift that occurred in my energy system during the META-Health course had an immediate impact on his energy system, because virtually the moment I got home, he finished with me! I didn't have to do anything at all. I had already done my work on the course. I believe he immediately, across space and time, picked up on my energy shift, and his decision to leave, on some level, was because he knew I wasn't the same. And I wasn't.

What I experienced allowed me to take a massive step forward in terms of moving out of my overwhelming sadness. My energy changed, and because it was connected to his through the universal field, he felt it. I appreciate that this may all sound a bit hard to believe, but that is exactly what happened. Energy is fascinating, and the more you understand it, the crazier it can get. All I ask is that you stay open-minded, and in the next few chapters, you will see how your energy system plays an integral part in your healing.

Energy and spirituality

I'll delve a little deeper now, and discuss a more spiritual aspect of loss in relation to us all as energetic beings. Einstein's discovery, mentioned earlier, that energy cannot be created or destroyed – it can only change form – may be more relevant to life and death than we realise. Is it that our deceased loved ones have moved from their seemingly solid physical state to another that we do not fully understand? If we follow this to its logical conclusion, that means when someone dies, it is not the end. What if death, instead of being an end, is rather a transferral of the energy of our physical life to a state of pure energy? Could this transcendent state be evidence of what some religions, spiritual gurus, and ancient mystics refer to as the *soul* energy, or simply the *soul*?

What if, in life, we are not a physical body simply having a physical experience, but rather we are a soul having a human experience? As the human experience comes to an end, we simply return to our natural state of soul.

Just consider the possibility that because we aren't aware of this concept, and have been through years of cultural, social, and family conditioning, we have come to see death as *losing* someone, when in actual fact they are not lost at all and have just transmuted into another form and are still very much with us. It is certainly worth thinking about. This view may sit very comfortably with you, or it may not resonate with you at all. My aim here is not to try and convince you of anything, but instead to help you to think about your loss in a way that is most comfortable and healing for you. However, the most important thing is to be true to what you heart feels. In no way is this meant to question any personal religious beliefs you may have. Rather, it is an exploration of how energy can affect our grief.

I have worked with many, many people who have been devastated by the loss of a loved one, and of those who have integrated their grief using the techniques described in this book, nearly all of them said that they felt a closer connection to their loved ones. There is potential to feel a new sense of connection – one that is often shattered by our engrained belief that we are all separate. While I will be discussing beliefs in chapter 8, here I will expand on the energy aspect of connection. There are several simple methods and tools which can help to explore that connection.

The energy of crystals and colour

In the self-love exercises at the end of this chapter, you will be introduced to both crystals and colour: two powerful energy providers that can help you wherever you are in your grieving process. Their power is significant. Historically they have both played major roles in healing both body and mind.

Crystals have been shown time and time again to have very specific energetic properties, with each individual crystal having its own unique quality. As long as humans have been on this Earth, they have had some affinity with stones and have used them throughout the years for various purposes. For example, the first Baltic amber amulets, some as many as 30,000 years old, were found to have been used in Britain around 10,000 years ago, likely as a means of protection against evil spirits. The Egyptians wore them as jewellery for both protection and health, as did the ancient Greeks. Soldiers were said to have rubbed hematite over their bodies before battles for protection. The Chinese have used jade for around 1,000 years, both as protection and as a kidney-healing stone.

Crystals have also been referred to in many religious texts from around the world, including the Bible and the Koran, and have played a role in the religious practices of both Buddhists and Hindus. Even during the Renaissance, crystals and herbs were still being utilised for healing purposes, and while they are no longer accepted by mainstream medicine, they have been continually used in many cultures across the world. Having studied crystals for three years, I have certainly seen how powerful they can be, which is why I have included them as part of this *Self-Love* section.

Colour is another form of healing energy. Like crystals, it has been helping people for many, many thousands of years. In ancient Egypt, China, India, and Greece, phototherapy (light therapy) was used, and according to Egyptian mythology, the art of chromotherapy (use of colour to cure diseases) was discovered by the god Thoth. Avicenna, a physician and philosopher born in 980 AD, advanced the use of colour in both the diagnosis and treatment of illness. He even developed a chart which related colour to the temperature and the physical condition of the body. Throughout the nineteenth century, colour was used and studied by many researchers in relation to the health of the body. One popular way of using colour today is through a system developed by Melissa Jolly called 'Colour Mirrors', where you choose a bottle containing coloured essential oils and through interpretation, the colours can reflect back to you your attributes and possible blocks to your happiness. Please see the *Resources* section for more information on this. Some people have even described colour as the language of the soul.

Joy Beyond Grief – Self-Love Exercises

Crystal meanings and exercises

Crystals can be bought from specialist shops, online or from my website. I sell all of the specific crystals I discuss here in a single pack, with the instructions for the layout described below. www.janicethompson.co.uk

Here are some crystal suggestions that are particularly helpful during grief.

Rose Quartz – a crystal of the heart. It can help release the shock of grief; it is a stone which encourages self-love. It can soothe inner pain and help to invoke self-trust and self-forgiveness.

Mangano Calcite – also a crystal of the heart. It helps release fear and grief, and brings in unconditional love. It is a loving energy and helps in times of trauma. It also helps lift anxiety and tension from the body.

Apache Tear – a comforter in times of grief. It is excellent for absorbing negative energy.

Amethyst – a crystal which encourages spiritual wakefulness. It helps quieten the mind and promotes inner peace. It is particularly helpful during grief and loss, and if you put it under your pillow, it will help you to sleep better. It can also be worn for long periods, such as throughout grieving.

Smokey Quartz – a crystal which can help with stress. It is classically known as the anti-stress stone. It also helps us cope with sorrow. It has a relaxing effect on the body, and helps relieve fear and lift depression. It is one of the most effective grounding stones there is. It can be worn for long periods of time.

Be sure to run your crystals under cold water regularly to cleanse them. If you would like more information on how crystals can help with your grief, please feel free to contact me.

Below are some ideas for working with crystals. Simply do your heart breathing exercise, and while keeping your focus on your heart, try working with one of the following exercises.

- Simply choose a crystal which appeals to you most in the moment (using your intuition), and that will be the right stone for you to carry for the day, or longer if it feels right (you could wear it as a pendant).
- Choose a crystal to place under your pillow at night.
- Sit quietly for a while and focus on the crystal, its colour, and texture. You can hold it to a certain part of your body for as long as feels comfortable.
- Using your intuition, choose a few crystals and make a mandala (arrange them in a pattern), and then sit quietly, focusing on that pattern for a while, or simply leave it somewhere for you to view.
- You can listen to my crystal meditation on my website: www. janicethompson.co.uk
- Try the crystal layout below. I have devised it specially to help with the pain of grief. (This is the layout pack I mentioned above that you can buy from my website.)

THE CRYSTAL LAYOUT

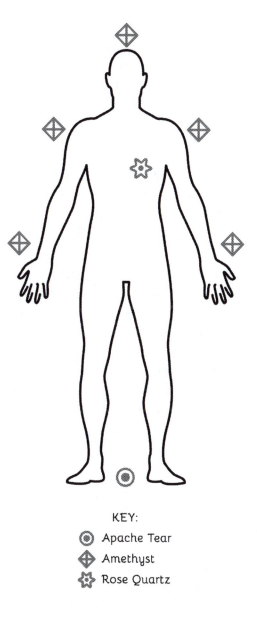

KEY:
- ◉ Apache Tear
- ◈ Amethyst
- ✾ Rose Quartz

Additionally, you could see a crystal therapist if it feels right. The therapist will work with specific crystals to help you with your grief. Please see the *Resources* section for more information.

Or perhaps you are more attracted to colours. If so, the following information and exercises are for you.

Colour meanings and exercises

Red – associated with the root chakra. It stimulates activity and is also energising. It can stimulate your inner fire and can evoke strong emotions.

Orange – associated with the sacral chakra. It energises and helps you to focus. It has a vitalising effect on the body, and can promote happiness and enhance creativity. It helps us find harmony and balance and brings joy to life. It also helps with transitions in life.

Yellow – associated with the solar plexus. It rejuvenates and helps regulate the nervous system and the immune system. It also balances the mind. It can have a cheering effect, and promotes a positive attitude to life. It can also help overcome depression.

Green – associated with the heart chakra. It is known for its healing properties and helps balance emotions and relationships. It deals with all matters of the heart. It has an effect on emotions by releasing them or intensifying them. It helps to discharge anger and promote inner peace, balance and enthusiasm. It is described as the energy of love and transformation.

Blue – associated with the throat chakra. It helps with self-communication and communication with others. It has a cooling and calming effect on the body, encouraging relaxation and openness. It helps overcome fear and promotes a flow by helping us to recognise our barriers.

Indigo – associated with the third eye chakra. It is linked with heightened perception, intuition, and can promote a deep sense of connection and peace. It has a cleansing effect, and helps in times of sorrow and trauma. It helps us awaken to our deep, innate knowledge of ourselves while promoting inner calm.

Purple – associated with the crown chakra. It is the colour of transformation and is said to provide a link between the spiritual and the physical world. It stimulates creativity and imagination, particularly where the future is concerned. It helps to harmonise the mind and emotions.

White, *Gold*, and *Clear* – connected to universal energy. They have the potential to reflect all energies. They stimulate cleansing and clarity. These colours do not absorb light; they only reflect it, meaning that they are neutral and help bring the light to us. They help to clarify ideas, and are a great help in creating different possibilities for a brighter future.

Pink – pushes things forward subtly and in a soothing way. This is a peaceful colour, and helps to create harmony in the heart. Pink represents compassion, nurturing, and tenderness, and is often called the colour of universal love.

Black – promotes grounding and anchors energies. It absorbs light and is therefore good for helping to clear the excess energy of a blockage. It helps with resilience (helpful in times of grief). It helps us concentrate on the important and essential things of life.

So, what do you do with these colours? You can use them in several ways. Use your intuition as you make your decisions. Do your heart breathing and then decide which one you will try. Remember, there is no right or wrong, and the more you begin to trust your intuition (also known as listening to your heart), the happier you will feel with your own choice.

- You could wear the colour that feels healing to you on a particular day.
- You could go to a material shop and choose a colour which feels right for you by listening to your heart. Purchase a piece of that material approximately two metres in length, lay out your crystals on it and even lie alongside them on the material.

- You could sit and wrap some material or an item of clothing around yourself that is a soothing colour, and imagine it is a coloured blanket that holds you.
- You could do your heart breathing exercise and imagine breathing in a particular colour.
- Imagine lying in a bath or pool of coloured water.
- Follow the meditation below, which you can also listen to on my website: www.janicethompson.co.uk

Find a quiet place where you will not be disturbed for at least 10 minutes, and either sit or lie down. Ensure that you are warm or cool enough, and that you are wearing comfortable clothing.

Gently close your eyes and allow your body to relax into the position you have chosen. Shift your awareness to your breathing, and then focus on your heart breathing, in and out of your heart.

Imagine you are standing under a beautiful waterfall. You feel totally safe and in control of the flow of water, turning it up to really invigorate yourself, or turning it down a bit to a calm flow, or even a trickle if you prefer. The gentle water is cascading down onto your body, and you feel it gently soothe your muscles, flowing from your head down to your feet, and away over the smooth rocks.

Gradually, the water turns the colour of your choice, and as it gently flows over you, you gain all you need from that colour. Then, the colour changes, and a new colour flows over your body, with its specific qualities giving you all you need. When that feels complete, another colour flows over your body, gently cascading from your head down to your toes.

Finally, pure gold flows over you, allowing for that universal energy to fill your body with high vibrational energy, which will help with the difficult time you are facing at the moment. It truly is a deep cleansing for you, so keep in the moment and enjoy filling yourself with this pure energy.

Gradually, the water stops, and the warm sun dries you instantly. You are feeling warm and peaceful. Gently begin to move your fingers and toes, and become aware of the room you are in. Slowly open your eyes. Take your time getting up, and drink some water. Don't go rushing on to something else. Give yourself time and come back into your day slowly.

You can now look up which colours you chose, and see if their meanings are significant to you.

Additionally, you could see a colour mirror therapist if it feels right. A colour mirror therapist has been trained to use colour via a system of 100 bottles and essences, which are used to help with many of life's problems, including grief and loss. Please see the *Resources* section for more information.

Note: The crystal and colour exercises can be used with children.

Chapter 6

TIME WILL NOT HEAL,
BUT TAPPING WILL

'Some day the medical profession will wake up and
realise that unresolved emotional issues are the main
cause of 85% of all illnesses. When they do, EFT will
be one of their primary healing tools ... as it is for me.'
Dr Eric Robins

THERE IS AN OLD SAYING in loss, that 'time will heal'. From my experience, personally and professionally, time heals nothing. Don't get me wrong, as time passes and you get further away from your loss, things will feel different. However, any trapped energy from the shock of your loss, any specific troublesome memories you may have, or anything that could retrigger the pain can affect you at any time. I have seen anger surface seemingly out of the blue. I have seen people beating themselves up over and over for what initially looked like a trivial issue. All these people had what I call 'unresolved grief'. Unless you do something to clear any trapped energy within your system, many, many years can pass without time having healed your loss. Your initial pain might well have dissipated, but the energy from that pain is only a trigger away. Remember, a trigger can be one of many aspects frozen around the time of your loss, and can have the potential to reignite old, painful feelings regularly.

For example, my mother never got over my father's death, and subsequently became more and more bitter about life, taking it out on those around her whose husbands were still alive. For my mother, anyone and everyone's husband was a trigger that took her straight back to the pain and bitterness she felt over her husband being 'taken away', as she would say. In other instances, people may suffer from a physical issue which they will not have even associated with their loss all those years before. For example, I had a client who was diagnosed with rheumatoid arthritis not long after he lost his wife. When I worked with him some ten years afterwards, we established a connection between his loss and his condition.

If you are just looking to be numbed, time may help, but you can help yourself so much better than that: you really can. I urge you not to sit back and wait for time to pass. Be active, and keep doing what you are doing, and don't stop reading and following the exercises in this book.

One time, a client came through my door and literally broke down, barely making it to the chair. She was overcome with emotion, and she was crying so hard that she was struggling to breathe. I sat by her and asked her to focus on her heart area, and we did some heart breathing. I asked this lady if I could tap on her. She nodded, and I began tapping – also known as Emotional Freedom Techniques (EFT). No words, apart from the occasional reminder from me to breathe through her heart. This went on for a short time until her crying subsided, at which point we began talking about how I might be able to help her. This is an example of how EFT can truly help calm someone down before I even begin to help them with the issue that they came to me with.

My initial experience of tapping (EFT)

My own initial experience with EFT was with Karl Dawson, an EFT master and the creator of *Matrix Reimprinting*, which is discussed in the next chapter. I came into the room and took a seat. Throughout the morning, I watched Karl work with others on the course, many of whom became quite emotional. I thought, 'That wouldn't be me; I am in control of my emotions. I am not going to show any vulnerability!' – all very old, learnt ways of thinking, which I now know are not very helpful when trying to feel better. Oh, how wrong was I!! I can't remember the exact reason why he came over to me – maybe something that someone said had triggered me into thinking about Andy's death – but he could see that something was up. What I experienced for the next fifteen minutes or so was absolutely amazing, unimaginable. I began to talk about Andy and how much I missed him, and how deeply sad I was. I began to sob and shake a lot as Karl tapped on me, but after a while I started to feel better, and I felt that something had *shifted*. (I use this term all the time now, to describe the feeling I get when I know something has changed within my very being.) I knew I was going to be all right – something I really hadn't felt before.

This is something my clients often say happens to them when we have done some work together. It's hard to describe, but something just feels different and lighter inside. I was quite exhausted afterwards, but I truly felt like a weight had been lifted off my shoulders. I do owe many thanks to my good friend Karl.

So, what actually happened when Karl started tapping on me? He could see that I was distraught, and immediately started tapping as I had done on the client I mentioned earlier. This had a direct effect on my energy system, which is what tapping is designed to do. As the immense energy of my shock began to be released, my body began to shake quite a lot. This was the trapped energy of the shock being discharged from my body. Remember that when energy gets released from a trauma, the body can shake. I could feel something being released.

After that session, I began to notice that I was not getting emotionally triggered back to the shock of Andy's death. Two things happened. Firstly, I did not think of his death as much, and secondly, when I did, the feeling was far more neutral. Instead of my mind always going back to the moment of his death, I would think of happy memories, and times when we enjoyed each other's company. This was such a nicer place to go to, and one which was a true reflection of our lives together. I was able to reflect far more easily on the twenty years of wonderful memories, as opposed to the terrible few hours surrounding his death. His life, our relationship, and our love are what I now recall.

To help yourself through your loss, with all the pain and negative emotions related to it, let's see it in terms of a disturbance in your energy system, caused by your loss via the painful emotions you are experiencing. Let's help you in this chapter with the use of tapping to restore balance, thereby easing the pain and bringing your happier memories to the forefront.

What is tapping (EFT)?

EFT was developed by Gary Craig and evolved from a therapy called Thought Field Therapy, developed by Dr Roger Callahan. It grew and has become known around the world. EFT has been described as acupuncture without needles. Both acupuncture and EFT use acupoints, which are part of the network of energy lines found throughout the body – the meridians, as we discussed earlier. EFT uses the fingers to tap (or rub, if you prefer) on some specific acupoints, thereby creating motion which helps energy flow and clears any blockages. For every point you tap on, there is an associated organ and a body system related to that organ. Whether physical problems are experienced depends on the severity of the emotional issue in terms of intensity, or how long it has been affecting the body (suffering). Tapping helps clear the blockage, and as the energy begins to flow again, the recipient feels better on all levels. So, can you see how crucial it is to have a healthy energy system? It affects every other system in your body. A healthy energy system will lead to a healthy physical, emotional, mental, and spiritual state.

EFT works from the premise that any negative emotion is a disturbance in the body's energy system. When you experience anything that causes you stress, this energy system can become blocked, and by tapping on it you can clear the blockage. Your guide to knowing that your energy system is blocked is recognising how you are feeling. Sad, angry, disconnected – those feelings all mean there's a block. Now, don't get me wrong here, you are feeling all the emotions you are feeling because you are hurting and that is totally normal. It is only when those emotions get stuck that problems arise.

If you have recently been bereaved, those feelings are going to be raw; tapping will help by easing them just a little bit. This practical tool can be extremely beneficial, as it gives you some power back as you help yourself with the intensity of difficult feelings. If you are still struggling with a bereavement from some time ago, those emotions may have become stuck, and tapping will help clear the blockage. Remember back to the chapter on pain, suffering, and letting go, when I said you would not be human if you didn't feel pain when you lost a loved one? If you are still suffering years later, it is not so healthy. Tapping is about minimising and managing that pain – understanding its potential and transforming it into something special. After acknowledging your problem, we choose what is known as a *set-up* phrase, which is a description of the problem followed by a self-acceptance statement. Acceptance of yourself is also a crucial part of EFT. For example, say you are using your *Healing Heart*, and after deciding to work on feeling really heartbroken, you find that you scored -6. Then, the set-up phrase could be, 'Even though I am feeling heartbroken, I love and accept myself'. If you find it a challenge to say 'I love and accept myself', you could instead say, 'I'm OK', or if that doesn't feel right, maybe try, 'I'm here'.

With EFT, it is very important to use the language and words that feel right for you, so that you can really tune in, saying the words out loud wherever possible. If you do find it a continual challenge to say 'I love and accept myself', at some point it would be advisable to look at your own self-love, because if you find it hard to say those words, it is because they are having some impact on you. Self-love, or the lack of it, can play a major role in loss.

After you have decided on your set-up phrase, you say it three times while tapping on one specific point. Next, move around each of the other points, just saying a shorter version – for example, 'My broken heart'. All will be explained in detail in the self-help section at the end of this chapter, where you will be able to try EFT for yourself. For now, it is important to know you can use EFT for any of the feelings you are experiencing that you perceive as negative. If you are questioning whether EFT works or not, you can simply start with, 'Even though I don't know if this is going to work, I totally love and accept myself', or, 'Even though I feel stupid tapping, I am OK'. The beauty of EFT is that you really can use tapping for everything.

Before beginning tapping, you need to give your problem an intensity. For the purposes of this book, it is scored between -10 and 0 (where -10 is the most intense feeling ever, and 0 is no intensity). Please refer to the grief scale in chapter 2. Why do this? As you tap, the intensity of the emotion will be reduced, and you will be able to give it a rating nearer to 0. This gives you something tangible to look for when assessing how you feel. It can be so reassuring in terms of having some control when overwhelmed with a strong, painful feeling.

A splash of research

If you are anything like me, you quite like to know some of the science/ research behind anything new. As this book goes to press, there are well over one thousand books for both adults and children on EFT, some forty-three randomised controlled studies, thirty-nine outcome studies and several case studies, all demonstrating over 98 per cent positive results.[1] There are conferences worldwide exploring the potential of EFT, and the pace of research is growing exponentially. EFTi (EFT international) is an organisation committed to clearly defining aims and objectives and maintaining strong codes of ethics and practices, and has current research and ways of incorporating EFT into the NHS which are accessible to all. Additionally, the EFT and Mindfulness Centre have research available on their website. (Please see the *Resources* section.) There are also several prominent researchers throughout the world who are consistently researching the benefits of EFT, such as Dawson Church, Dr Peta Stapleton, David Feinstein and Elizabeth Boath.

Although no direct studies have been conducted with grief, there have been several studies where grief is a factor. For example, war veterans with PTSD (post-traumatic stress disorder) often encounter some form of grief and have been shown to have benefited from EFT.[2,3] Studies with those experiencing stress,[4] depression[5] and anxiety[6] – all of which those struggling with grief may experience – have also shown positive outcomes when using EFT.

Research shows physiological changes with EFT. In a study of war veterans with PTSD, each of the 203 subjects received 10 hour-long sessions of EFT. Their bodies were tested before and after for changes in interleukins (genes which are responsible for regulating the body's inflammation response; inflammation has been shown to be associated with PTSD).[7] Results showed that the inflammation response had significantly decreased following their sessions. Additionally, "good" genes associated with improved functioning of the immune system were upregulated.[8]

With regards to PTSD, there is a very well-made film which shows how EFT helped several war veterans back to physical and mental health. It is called *OPERATION: Emotional Freedom – The Answer*. A short clip of this inspirational film can be seen by following the link in the *Resources* section.

There is also a study conducted in Rwanda in 2008, published in *Energy Psychology: Theory, Research and Treatment*, in which EFT was found to reduce psychological symptoms of complex PTSD within two groups of orphaned genocide survivors.[9] A 37.3 per cent reduction in symptoms was recorded, and 40 per cent dropped below the clinical cut-off point for PTSD at a six-month follow-up. These findings are consistent with other findings regarding EFT and PTSD, and clearly show that EFT is beneficial in times of grief and shock.

In addition to the formal research, more and more celebrities are using EFT – Lily Allen, Madonna, and Michael Ball are among those who have talked about it; various athletes are using it for improved sports performance. Go to the *Resources* section to find out about more research.

The benefits of using EFT with grief

I cannot sing EFT's praises enough as a tool that you can use to help yourself. With your own grieving experience, it can help you in several different ways – not least of all because it uses no drugs or equipment. It can be used alongside any medications you may be currently taking. It is a safe, painless, and gentle technique. EFT is non-invasive and is easily learnt, and you don't even have to believe in it for it to work. It doesn't cost anything, either. It is an excellent tool to use for all aspects of grief, and for everyone experiencing it.

All of the above benefits are enough to warrant giving EFT a try, but there is an even more fundamental reason why I recommend that you use it. It can help you to feel better than you do, right now! It can help in any one of those moments of intense pain, which hopefully you have included on your *Healing Heart*. Literally, as and when these feelings arise, you can tap on them. EFT is your own personal little helper – your own self-help tool that you have access to 24/7.

You can also use it with friends and family. It can be extremely beneficial to tap together, and it is a brilliant tool to help grieving children. I would also strongly recommend your grief buddy learns it, too. They can tap with you. This is an excellent way for them to support you, and they can also remind you to tap if you are so absorbed by your feelings that you forget all about it, which can happen. They will be benefiting on some level, too.

One of EFT's main advantages is that it helps you to feel more in control of what is happening to you. Grief can be so overwhelming, with any number of difficult feelings to deal with, and with death often comes uncertainty and fear. These can lead to feelings of unpredictability, where fear of a loss of control is common. Having a technique that you can use at any time will aid you in feeling a little bit more in control. Often, loss can stir feelings of your own mortality, which can be frightening, but guess what? You can tap on that, too! You can tap on anything that makes you feel uncomfortable – anything at all. EFT it is an empowering tool, and one which you are in complete control of.

EFT can be used at any time in the grieving process. Regardless of whether you have been bereaved over the last few days, or if you were bereaved many years ago, it is all about unblocking your energy system from whenever it became blocked. This is the absolute beauty of EFT for grief. It doesn't matter where you are in your grieving experience, you will be able to use it to help yourself.

How to use EFT for grief

EFT can help in two major ways – as a self-help tool, which I highly recommend, and also as a technique to be used with a trained practitioner, which I will talk more about later.

Why use EFT on yourself?

One of the reasons why I asked you to fill in the *Grieving Hearts* earlier in the book was to help you to own your specific emotions, so that when you got to this part in the book you would have a clear understanding of what would be beneficial for you to tap on. Perhaps naming how you feel is easy; perhaps naming emotions may be very difficult. If the latter describes you, keep using the *Grieving Hearts* to help. You don't actually have to name your emotion in terms of anger, helplessness, or guilt. You can just know it's that crushing feeling in your chest, and tap on it. Or maybe it is that dull ache in your heart? Tap on that. Perhaps it is that wrenching feeling in your gut? You guessed it – tap on that too.

It is the tuning into your feelings, and not trying to run or hide from them, that is important in moving through your grief in a healthy way. Now, I am not suggesting that you look at your feelings 24/7, but recognising what emotions you are experiencing when they show up, and doing something positive about relieving them, is 100 per cent what I am suggesting. OK, so what if you are out doing your shopping, or filling the car with petrol when you become overwhelmed with emotion? How do you tap then? Good point! Personally, I would actually tap anywhere now, but that is because I have been doing it for such a long time that I feel if something is going to help me, I am going to do it regardless of how mad I look! I fully appreciate that if this is all new to you, tapping in public may be a tap too far. However, you could always choose one point to tap on discreetly, as an emergency point. This is described in the *Self-Love* section at the end of this chapter.

As mentioned earlier, a brilliant advantage of EFT as a self-help tool is that your friends and family can tap with you. Let's say, for example, you are having a chat with a friend, and you become overwhelmed with immense sadness. You can ask them to tap along with you, or if a child becomes upset, you can either tap on them or tap along with them. There is something called 'borrowed benefits' in EFT, which means that if you tap along with someone, you can gain the benefits of tapping even though it is the other person's issue you are tapping on. If you are with someone close to you, chances are that they will also have been affected by the loss, so tapping can help you both. Tapping together can also be a bonding experience. When I run my courses, the whole group taps along with whomever I am working with. It can help them feel supported and the group to feel connected.

EFT is also brilliant for grieving children. Please encourage them to do some tapping, too. Often, children are more receptive to it than adults because they don't have as many years of engrained scepticism under their belts. You can just explain how to tap, and they get on with it. You can tap along with your children, and you will all benefit, both emotionally and through bonding. In chapter 1, I discussed the fact that when my father died, I did not have much emotional support. If I had only known about EFT, I believe I would have had much less of a hard time. Since I have used EFT, I have encouraged my two daughters to use it whenever they need to, and this certainly came in handy when our springer spaniel was found dead on the main road a few metres from our house. Almost immediately, I sat down with the girls and we all tapped together on the emotions we were feeling. It helped all of us to deal with the shock and sadness, and definitely made us feel connected and supportive of each other. It felt like something positive we could do in that moment. Before I had the knowledge of EFT, I would have probably done what so many people do, and tried to get my girls doing something to take their minds off what had happened. I am so glad I had a far better approach available to me. You will have that too by the end of the chapter.

Working with an EFT practitioner

As I mentioned, EFT can be used with a trained practitioner. You can find a qualified practitioner either on the EFTi website: https:// eftinternational.org/discover-eft-tapping/find-eft-practitioners/ or the EFT and Mindfulness Centre website: https://www.eftandmindfulness.com/

Though there are likely to be professional practitioners listed in your area, you may feel that you wish to work with someone who is not local to you. If this is the case, rest assured, as most practitioners are happy to conduct sessions via Skype, FaceTime, Zoom or any other video conferencing platforms.

Working with a practitioner is beneficial for several reasons. It can help to have someone there with you as a source of support and guidance, and with their expertise, they can help you relate to your grief on a deeper level. They can certainly help with the most traumatic aspects of grief, such as shock and intense emotions, along with any other particularly upsetting or frightening events associated with your loss. Additionally, they can help you with any feelings of resentment or regret. As I've mentioned before, maybe you didn't say something you wish you had, or maybe you acted in a way you wish you hadn't. These are but a few possible issues that may still be weighing heavily on your mind, and would benefit from work with a practitioner.

But now, it is time for you to experience EFT for yourself.

Joy Beyond Grief – Self-Love Exercise

I invite you to join me for some EFT. There are a couple of ways in which you can do this, so choose whichever is most comfortable for you. You can either use your *Healing Heart* or, if you are feeling particularly emotional at the moment, you can work with that emotion. I suggest trying both options at different times.

SELF-HELP TAPPING POINTS

Below are the abbreviations and descriptions of the tapping points I use.

TAPPING POINTS	LOCATION
Side of the hand (SH)	Side of the hand
Top of Head (TH)	Middle of the top of the head (imagine if you were pulling on a string directly in the centre of the head)
Eyebrow (EB)	Beginning of the eyebrow, nearest the nose
Side of Eye (SE)	On the bone at the outer side of the eye
Under Eye (UE)	On the bone under the eye, in line with the centre of the eye
Under Nose (UN)	Between the nose and upper lip
Under Lip (UL)	Under the bottom lip and above the chin, halfway between the two
Collar Bones (CB)	On the collarbones, towards where they meet, feel the knobbly part and drop your fingers 45 degrees into the small dips
Under Arm (UA)	Where a bra strap would be, level with the nipples
Thumb (TH)	On the outer edge of the thumbnail
Index Finger (IF)	On the outer edge of the index fingernail
Middle Finger (MF)	On the outer edge of the middle fingernail
Ring Finger (RF)	On the outer edge of the ring fingernail
Little Finger (LF)	On the outer edge of the little finger

You can now practise some tapping on your own, following the order shown above. You should tap about 7 times on each of the points shown in the diagram below:

THE TAPPING POINTS

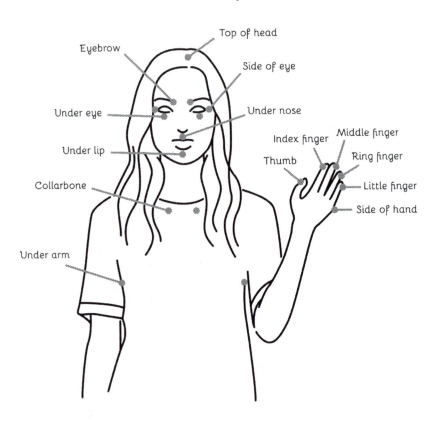

You have now familiarised yourself with the points, and you know which order to tap in. Please practise until you are comfortable with each point. You could initially start with some deep breaths as you tap on each point.

So, now we will see exactly how and when to use these tapping points to help yourself. You could also go to my website and follow the video of me tapping, and you can tap along with me.

Tapping with the Healing Heart

Step 1 - Using your *Healing Heart*, start by selecting one of your emotions which is in the middle area of your heart around the -5 -0 area. The reason why I am asking you to select an emotion from here, and not one of your most intense emotions, is to allow you to start working on your emotions gradually. Only when you feel completely confident, or when working with a practitioner, should you move on to your more intense emotions.

Step 2 - Simply acknowledge the intensity of that emotion from how you scored it on your *Healing Heart:* from between -10 to 0 (-10 being the most intense feeling, and 0 being no intensity). It is important to note here that at this moment the emotion may be more or less intense than you originally recorded it to be. That is fine, you can simply re-score the emotion and carry on.

Step 3 - Once you are familiar with the tapping points and sequence (at the beginning of the *Self-Love* exercises in this chapter), begin with tapping on the SH point while saying, 'Even though I feel (say the emotion you chose here), I am OK'. Repeat this 3 times. Then, going around each of the points, say, 'This (say the emotion here)'. For example, 'This anger/sadness/crushing feeling in my chest'. Tap at least 7 times on each point while repeating the emotion, and then move on to the next point until you reach your little finger.

Step 4 - Re-rate your original intensity. Is it the same or has it gone down? Has it gone up, or has it changed into another emotion? If it is the same or has gone up, do another few rounds. If it has gone down, great. You will get used to assessing where it feels OK to bring it down to, but I suggest you keep tapping until it has gone down nearer to -2. Sometimes, the emotion changes while tapping, so go with the new emotion if that happens. For example, you begin by tapping on anger, but then the feeling changes to sadness. In that case, just change your word to *sadness* instead of *anger*. You do not need to start again. Just continue from wherever you are, at whichever point that is.

Using an emotion you are feeling right now

Step 1 - If you are experiencing a negative emotion right now, you can use it instead of one from your *Healing Heart*. Simply name the emotion or feeling, for example, 'this sadness' or 'this aching in my heart'.

Step 2 - Now rate the intensity of that emotion from -10 to 0 (-10 being the most intense feeling, and 0 being no intensity), the same way you did in your *Healing Heart*. You could even add this feeling/emotion to that chart if you want to, if it's not there already.

Repeat Steps 3 and 4 from *Tapping with the* Healing Heart.

You now have a wonderful technique to use in conjunction with your *Healing Heart*, and you can also use it whenever you feel any negative emotion. You can print off the tapping points and keep them with you, should you need to remind yourself of them.

Tapping for Letting Go

In chapter 4, we discussed letting go, and in the *Self-Love* section at the end, I asked you to ask yourself the following questions:

1. At this moment in time, am I able to let this feeling go?
2. Is it OK for this feeling to be here?
3. How does this feeling serve me?
4. Am I afraid of letting it go?

You can now use tapping for any of the answers you gave that indicate something you may need some help with. For example, if for question 1 you answered, 'No, I do not feel I can let this anger go', you can do tapping on it, saying, 'Even though I do not feel I can let this anger go, I am OK'.

Repeat this 3 times on the SH point, and then go around each of the points saying again, 'I do not feel I can let this anger go'. You can replace 'this anger' with whatever it is you feel you cannot let go of.

Whatever you answered for each question, you can tap on it if it feels negative or uncomfortable. Here are some examples. 'Even though it is not comfortable for this ... feeling to be here, I'm OK' or 'Even though this guilt doesn't serve me, I don't know how to let it go. I am OK'. Repeat 3 times on the SH point, and then go around each of the points, saying again, 'It is not OK for this ... feeling to be here' or 'This guilt doesn't serve me, I don't know how to let it go'. By being very specific with words, you are fine-tuning your tapping and this is important to help you move through any feelings of letting go which are bothering you. You may get some insight into what is behind your feelings, and be able to clear any specific blocks and let go of some feelings that are no longer serving you.

Tap and distract

Please be gentle with yourself, and do not force anything. Letting go of pain and stuck emotions and the way they present themselves is such an individual thing. If you are working alone and at any point you become distressed, I suggest you use the tap and distract technique. Definitely keep tapping, but take your attention away from what you are tapping on. Stop talking and focus on your heart breathing or your surroundings until you feel calm. Make a note of whatever it was that upset you, and seek help with this from a practitioner, as it may be too difficult for you to cope with on your own. Getting your grief buddy to tap with you can be reassuring and helpful too.

Emergency tapping point

It can be very helpful to have what is known as an emergency tapping point – just one of the tapping points that you can tap on in situations where you are unable to do the full sequence. Maybe you're on a crowded train, or talking one-to-one with someone. If you choose one point, you can discreetly tap on it. The finger points are good for this, as you can simply tap your thumb on the outside of your index finger on the same hand. Please use your emergency point if a feeling becomes overwhelming and you are out and about. You always, then, will have a means to help reduce the intensity of a feeling.

You now have a practical, gentle, safe, and effective tool to use whenever you need it, so get tapping.

Note: Tapping can be used with children. (Please consult the *Resources* section for a rhyme I wrote to help children learn tapping. It also may be helpful to you if you have young children affected by loss.)

Chapter 7

RESOLVING THE UNRESOLVABLE

'Matrix Reimprinting is a new, cutting-
edge personal development technique which
drastically improves health and wellbeing.'
Karl Dawson

THIS CHAPTER IS ALL ABOUT upsetting memories. Those troublesome, heart-wrenching memories. Those memories that haunt you in the quiet of night. Memories that pop into your mind when you are least expecting them. Memories which, upon entering your conscious awareness, do one thing and one thing only – they make you feel bad. Hopefully, there will be beautiful memories, too, of the wonderful times spent with your loved one, and those will be cherished and called upon at the end of this chapter. Here, though, I wish to help you deal with those memories that are not helping you move forward at all, and that are keeping you stuck in your grief.

Ellen

Ellen lost her partner when she was young, after he had been poorly for some time with lung cancer. She came to see me around a year after he died, and we worked together through many different aspects of her loss. On one particular occasion, she explained how guilty she had felt about a time she had been to see him in hospital. It was a memory which would not go away. It was with her all the time, causing her considerable distress. She kept replaying over and over how, after she had taken her shoes off during the visit, her partner had tripped and fallen over them when he got up to go to the toilet. Even though he had not been badly hurt, the guilt she felt was overwhelming, because he had been so poorly, and she had been so careless.

We used the wonderful tool that is Matrix Reimprinting on this specific memory. We cleared the guilt, and she made total peace with the memory – so much so that when I mentioned it a few weeks later, to see if it was still troubling her, she had forgotten all about it. This was a memory that had been causing her so much heartache for more than a year. She had resolved the unresolvable, and even more importantly, she had more free space in her mind to recall those special, fun times she had shared with her partner, instead of constantly running this event over and over in her mind.

So, what is Matrix Reimprinting?

Matrix Reimprinting combines working in that invisible network of energy connecting us all and everything, which, as mentioned in chapter 5, is called 'the matrix' by many, and 'reimprinting', which involves changing imprints within this matrix which are no longer supporting your wellbeing.

Matrix Reimprinting is a groundbreaking, modern technique, which is a revolutionary way to deal with the pain of loss, as well as many other aspects of the grieving experience. It is a gentle, non-invasive process, which incorporates EFT. It works on an energetic level and is not a superficial experience. Rather, it is one that will enable the trapped negative emotions surrounding your loss to be released. It helps you gain an understanding of underlying beliefs, and then creates a positive experience, which helps to bring peace and a sense of hope. Another major benefit of this technique is that it not only allows you to work through any specific haunting memories, but by doing so you can make sense of other aspects of your loss.

I mentioned earlier that Karl Dawson created this technique. He is one of the most intuitive and innovative people I have ever had the pleasure of meeting and working with. Some years ago, while teaching EFT, he had somewhat of an *Aha* moment. He was working with a student, and at one point she recalled an incident from her childhood. She said, 'I could almost tap on that young child!' So she did and that was the beginning of the Matrix Reimprinting technique explained in this chapter.

Karl went on to write two books on the subject: one with Sasha Allenby: *Matrix Reimprinting Using EFT*, which explains the basics of the technique. More recently, he has co-authored *Transform Your Beliefs, Transform Your Life* with Kate Marillat. This is another must-read, as it clearly explains in great detail how Matrix Reimprinting can help with many issues. There is also a chapter dedicated to grief, to which I was delighted to make a contribution.

Matrix Reimprinting and EFT

Matrix Reimprinting, like EFT, works on the premise that all negative emotions are caused by disruptions to the body's energy system. Although Matrix Reimprinting incorporates the same tapping that you learnt in the previous chapter, the technique takes EFT a step further, in that it allows you to understand your underlying beliefs. It deals with any upsetting memories in a gentle way, and helps to replace stuck energy with positive energy.

In my opinion, the best time to utilise EFT is during the days immediately following loss, when emotions and feelings are most obviously pronounced. As previously explained, the gentle tapping can help reduce the intensity of these emotions. However, regarding specific memories, I recommend that you try Matrix Reimprinting.

How does Matrix Reimprinting work?

Matrix Reimprinting uses memories as a way to help resolve any shocks from loss, any stuck emotions, and any conscious or unconscious beliefs that aren't working for you. When these things are resolved, it allows for you to create a positive new picture of that memory. This is all done by working with that younger you from those memories. They may be very old memories from when you were a small child or more recent memories of a few weeks ago. When a memory troubles you, Matrix Reimprinting allows you to work with the you at the age of the memory. Karl invented a new term for this younger you, which is ECHO (**E**nergetic **C**onsciousness **HO**logram).

First, I need to tell you what an ECHO is. This is a part of Karl's genius and Matrix Reimprinting's effectiveness. An ECHO is the part of you that is formed when a shock occurs. A troublesome memory remains because the ECHO splits off at that moment of shock to help us survive. It splits off energetically, and literally holds all the information of that shock, as though freezing it in time.

Remember when we talked about the freeze response in chapter 3, where the body literally freezes, along with everything it's aware of in that moment? That is a survival mechanism, for by separating from that pain, we are able to continue with our lives. I believe that this is one of nature's amazing gifts, as it helps us to cope with trauma and shock; however, it also takes a lot of energy to hold all the information comprising such moments.

The concept of a part of us splitting off is nothing new. Soul retrieval has been a feature of spiritual movements dating back to ancient times, and many psychotherapists refer to a very distinct *inner child*. In psychology, the term *dissociation* is popular when discussing how people seek to separate themselves from the pain of trauma.

So, in my case, an ECHO was created at the exact time and date my husband died; one was also created when my dad died. Can you see when an ECHO may have been created in your life?

Using the memory of when my husband died as a way for you to understand how Matrix Reimprinting works, I will tell you about a session I had using Matrix Reimprinting. I imagined stepping into that memory, I saw my ECHO absolutely distraught so I imagined tapping on her. I didn't even try to talk to her at that point – I kept tapping on her for quite some time as she moved through her shock and lots and lots of different emotions. Eventually she became a lot calmer. I had cleared the feelings of shock and many of the attached emotions.

My ECHO was now able to communicate with me better. I imagined asking her if she had created any beliefs that day. I asked to find out whether this horrendous experience had caused me to create a belief. In my mind's eye, she said the following and I didn't see this coming, but it made complete sense when she said it. 'When anything good happens, something bad will happen.' I certainly had an *Aha* moment then myself. I saw a series of old memories that flashed before me of situations and events where I understood how that belief had become my reality. And I will say that some of those memories went back a long way. That belief had definitely impacted a large part of my life. It was a huge realisation.

After that, my ECHO wanted to say a proper goodbye to Andy, which I felt I had not been able to do due to the suddenness of his passing. This was a very private and spiritual moment for myself and my ECHO. I then invited Andy's soul into the picture I was imagining. We had the chance to say a calm, loving goodbye. It was a very special time. I then did what is known as the Reimprinting process – I placed a beautiful colour around the picture of our warm farewell. Then with all the new learning about my belief, I imagined taking that picture into my mind, through every neural pathway in my brain, down through the whole of my body. I imagined that picture going through every cell in my body and every system too. Then I took it into my heart and filled my heart with that calm, comforting picture. This felt particularly powerful. Finally, I imagined blasting it out into the universe.

More about ECHOs

You could have many ECHOs if you have had many traumas in your life. They don't have to be big traumas either and what's traumatic for you may not be for anyone else. But if something is traumatic for you, an ECHO will be formed. You could imagine them as lots of smaller yous all out in the matrix holding the pain, emotions and shock for you. Until such time as you work through them. Then gradually, as you do this, each of those ECHOs integrates back into you with all the new learnings – as in my example of finding out about my belief that when something good happens something bad will happen. With that knowledge and by changing that belief within the memory, the quality of my life has definitely improved. I no longer avoid enjoying myself and know why I was avoiding it before. For me, that old belief played out when I lost Andy, because he had been working away for a few years and had just moved back home, and I was so happy. Then he died – something bad happened. Now, knowing that these two things aren't related, I can be happy and it's OK.

You could look at these ECHOs as those freeze moments – all the energy of the trauma or loss held frozen in time, almost waiting to be resolved. By helping your ECHOs, you are helping yourself.

Reasons for using Matrix Reimprinting

Firstly, ECHOs carry the potential to affect you greatly at any time, through any number of environmental stimuli that could retrigger you. There are so many aspects in any one memory, and if you experience anything similar to any one of those aspects, you could plug straight back into the ECHO that is holding all the associated, fears, worries, pain, etc.

Additionally, the more ECHOs we have, the more the energy field around any beliefs within those ECHOs will grow, which may cause us to attract similar events into our lives via the law of attraction. I can name many occasions where my old belief of when something good happens then something bad will happen was played out in my life. Also, connections with all these ECHOs take a lot of energy to maintain and as we get older, this can be exhausting. Far better to resolve the trauma and integrate those ECHOs back into us.

Another reason to use Matrix Reimprinting involves any beliefs developed at the time of a loss/trauma. These beliefs are usually subconscious, but when tapping is used within Matrix Reimprinting, they come into conscious awareness and can then be dealt with. Why are these beliefs so important? Because these beliefs can impact your whole life. As Mahatma Gandhi famously said:

> *Your beliefs become your thoughts,*
> *Your thoughts become your words,*
> *Your words become your actions,*
> *Your actions become your habits,*
> *Your habits become your values,*
> *Your values become your destiny.*

Looking at beliefs is a crucial part of Matrix Reimprinting, for the very reason that Gandhi explains – they have such an impact on your life and destiny. So changing any unwanted beliefs is life transforming.

You also have the opportunity to make the memory more comfortable for you. For instance, if an ECHO resides in a room that isn't very pleasant, you can brighten the walls, add flowers, nice curtains – simple things like that. You can also make the picture as comfortable as possible by moving the memory around a bit. Conversations that were difficult can now be made easier to have; actions that were not taken can be included. Any disempowering beliefs that were formed that day can be resolved by replacing them with empowering beliefs. Ellen, whom I mentioned at the beginning of the chapter, visualised in her mind's eye speaking to her boyfriend about what had happened, and he told her that she was not a bad person – it was just an accident. She then felt resolution to this troublesome memory.

The technique not only deals with the trauma but it incorporates a positive aspect to support new beliefs. A new version of the memory is created with its own field of energy with supporting beliefs. Then the gentle, reaffirming Reimprinting process completes this technique.

The Reimprinting Process

When your new picture is the way you wish it to be, you are ready to reimprint this picture, as described earlier in my own experience. You imagine bringing this new picture into every cell in your body and through every neural pathway of your brain. Most crucially, we engage the power of the heart to help with this process. The heart is a huge player in the energetic world. It is the means by which we humans energetically interact with the matrix, which in turn connects us all. I discussed earlier the importance of the heart and how it is both electrically and magnetically stronger than the brain.

It is a powerful force, sending and receiving messages both to and from the brain and the environment. According to the HeartMath Institute, the heart is the medium through which information is relayed between the brain, the subconscious fields of our own energy systems, and the matrix. In Matrix Reimprinting, we bring in the new supportive pictures through the heart, into the body, and then send them out again into the matrix. We can then regularly recall that new picture, thereby reinforcing it.

Matrix Reimprinting and communication
with your deceased loved one

When working with Matrix Reimprinting, many people engage in a form of communication with their deceased loved ones. You can do this by inviting them into the picture you are working on and speak with them from this higher perspective – a perspective of a higher self. This often leads to a moment of enlightenment and much pain release. What do I mean by *higher self*? Our higher self could be simply described as our soul – the part of us that never dies. The part of us that is all-knowing. In my experience, if a client chooses to bring in the higher self of their loved one, there is typically much peace and love involved. It is more often than not a very powerful and helpful experience. However, it is not for everyone, and it is totally up to you whether or not you engage in this aspect of the technique.

My own example of Matrix Reimprinting at the beginning of the chapter shows how beautiful communication can be with the higher self of a deceased loved one. Below is an illustration of this.

Ellen

Returning to Ellen's story, once these feelings were dealt with, she then changed the room around a little bit to make it more comfortable for her partner in bed. She spoke with him, by connecting with his higher self in the picture, telling him how sorry she was, and explaining how much she loved him. He responded by reassuring her that she wasn't a bad person and that he totally understood it was an accident. This helped her ECHO to realise that it was not a problem for him. She could see it was simply an accident and wasn't because 'she couldn't get things right'. When she felt the picture was OK, and that the traumatic feelings had been cleared, and a new belief that she was, indeed, OK had been accepted, she reimprinted the picture, taking it into her heart and filling her whole body with it, before blasting it out into the matrix, the universe and beyond. After the session, she said that she felt totally different about the memory. The intensity of it had been taken away completely. Incidentally, she went on to produce a music album that she had previously 'not been able to get right'.

As discussed in chapter 1, emotional support and the connection with others is a very important part of moving through any grieving process. This is one reason (others will be discussed later in the chapter) why I would strongly recommend you work with a Matrix Reimprinting practitioner at least to start with. Matrix Reimprinting provides a natural and gentle platform to help support you, and a practitioner will guide you through each stage of the session. While we are never really disconnected from our deceased loved ones, it can certainly feel as though we are, as the physicality of them has gone. Matrix Reimprinting can help you to feel that connection again, albeit in a different way. During the sessions, there are always opportunities to invite the higher self of your loved one into the matrix, but additionally – and I feel this is so beautiful – the more pain in the form of trapped energy that is cleared, the closer many people feel to their lost loved ones. I know this has certainly been true for many of my clients, and also for myself. After my own personal Matrix Reimprinting experience, those buzzards certainly appeared more frequently for me.

Once the pain, shock, and trauma have been cleared, it is like a fog has lifted, and the connection and true loving feelings that were always there are seen again. This can feel like a reconnection to that part of our loved one, which was, is, and always will be there, but had been hidden behind the pain. We are always connected to our loved ones, as we are always connected to everything. It just feels so distant when we are hurting so much.

Not only can Matrix Reimprinting help with your feelings of connection to a deceased loved one – it can also help you to reconnect with yourself. Remember when I said that a part of you can split off following the shock of loss, creating an ECHO? Well, as your pain begins to subside, your ECHO no longer needs to hold onto the trauma for you, which means that the separated you can return with a new positive outlook. The more negative trapped energy you clear, the nearer you get to your true, heart-centred self.

Forgiveness and regret

Forgiveness can be such a large part of working with Matrix Reimprinting. Whilst working with their memory, I have seen many clients forgive themselves, others and/or their deceased loved ones.

Deirdre

Deirdre, who lost her baby brother when she was only seven, experienced forgiveness with Matrix Reimprinting. She not only helped her ECHO to work through her feelings of guilt and pain – she could also make peace with the issue for the first time in nearly fifty years. After working on her own guilt, and she felt a new kindness towards herself, another positive event occurred. Her next session began with 'You will never guess what has just happened to me!' She went on to tell me how, after years of cold relations with her mother that, for the first time ever that afternoon, her mother had tapped her on the leg and told her how much she cared about her, finally showing some true affection. This can often happen when working energetically with a person – others around them begin to act differently, too.

As well as being a great tool for helping with forgiveness of yourself and others, Matrix Reimprinting can also be used to help with regret. I am sure that you will be fully aware of any regrets you have regarding your loss. By dealing with these feelings, you will not be in a position of retriggering yourself at all and therefore will not be affected by any negative beliefs which may have formed. So if you are feeling regret about something done or not done, said or unsaid, what can you do?

With Matrix Reimprinting, you can go back to the specific time when you did or didn't do something that you wish you had or hadn't, and help your ECHO from that moment in time to resolve the issue. Allowing the negative emotions to be released will have a massive impact on that memory, and also provide you with peace of mind. This in turn can allow you to forgive yourself or others if necessary.

It may also be the case that the person who died did or said something to upset you, causing you lasting distress – which in itself could cause a problem. By using Matrix Reimprinting, you can go back in time to that memory and resolve what you have believed to be unresolvable. Speak to that person's higher self, and from my experience this will lead to positive change, as all of our higher selves are pure love.

Why deal with these troublesome memories?

So, what can happen if you don't clear these troublesome memories? Basically, they are going to hang around and cause a lot of misery. If you do not clear the trapped energy, that ECHO will hold onto the memory and its associated trauma. How will this affect you? Well, remember Gandhi's quote from earlier? You will form a belief around it, and eventually it will have such an effect on you that it will have the potential to become your destiny. It may show up again because something has retriggered it, and you will feel horrid. You may be consciously aware of this or you may not, especially if a lot of time has passed. In which case that link will be buried in your subconscious. I'll use my experiences as an example.

'I've been acting like a bloody rebellious teenager' is what I heard myself saying in a Matrix Reimprinting session sometime after losing my husband. It was then that the penny dropped. Yes, I was literally acting like a rebellious teenager, but why? As you may recall, my father died when I was fourteen years old, and because I had not dealt with that loss at the time, an ECHO had formed, comprised of all the trauma I'd suffered around my father's death. So, when Andy died some twenty-one years later, I was retriggered, and fell straight back into that same old behaviour. I not only formed a new ECHO (with the shock of Andy's death), but plugged straight back into my fourteen-year-old ECHO. I can tell you, it was not pretty.

For me, another very significant death had occurred, and my subconscious went straight back into what it knew – acting like a rebel. It had saved me all those years ago, and my subconscious thought it would save me again. However, this time I was an adult and rebelling wasn't helpful at all. Thanks to Matrix Reimprinting, I cleared the original and subsequent traumas, and now I am a totally different person for it. No need to rebel now, unless I choose to do so of course.

Is it possible that this splitting off – this ECHO, which holds the trauma – goes some way towards explaining why some people are literally stuck at a certain point in their lives? It is often a point of trauma that people cannot get past – constantly running a particular event over and over in their minds. I have met many clients who, not having dealt with their pain, are still suffering years later, and I've noticed that these people will often talk about their loss as if it only happened yesterday. In some cases, a retriggering can cause people to display signs of regressing back to the age they were at the time of their loss. Is that you? Well, it was certainly me! It really is as though you've found yourself stuck in a time warp.

When to use Matrix Reimprinting

Matrix Reimprinting can be utilised whenever you feel it is right. You may use it early on in your grieving experience, to help with specific issues, or you might pick it up as a tool to use six to twelve months after your loss. You may have just realised that some problems in your life are related to a loss which happened a long time ago. So, if you are still struggling with the pain and trauma of your loss, and feel that you are possibly being retriggered by some aspect of a past trauma which is reconnecting you with that ECHO, then why not try Matrix Reimprinting.

Why work with a practitioner?

Whilst this process is simple, and is possible to do on yourself, I would strongly recommend you work with a practitioner for several reasons. Firstly, they will tap on you, and you, energetically, will tap on your ECHO. This way of working enables you to focus on helping your ECHO. Trying to tap on yourself whilst imagining tapping on your ECHO can be somewhat of a challenge initially, but with the help of a practitioner, it is much simpler. The illustration below is a visual representation of a practitioner tapping on a client and a client tapping on their ECHO.

PRACTITIONER WORKING WITH A CLIENT

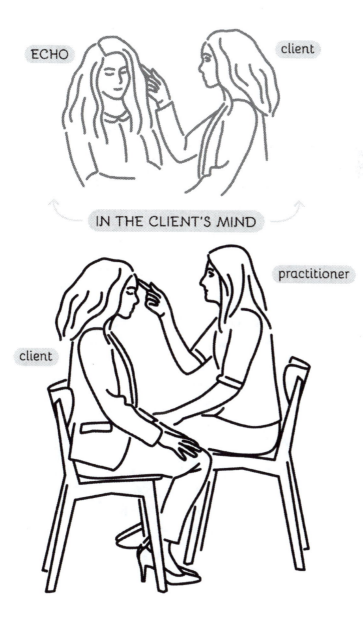

ECHO

client

IN THE CLIENT'S MIND

practitioner

client

A practitioner will guide you through the process, helping you to help your ECHO, and all the while ensuring that any trauma, shock, beliefs, or any other aspects that are troubling the ECHO are dealt with. They can also help if you get stuck with any aspect of the technique, and they are invaluable if you can't 'get out of your own way' so to speak. This often happens when working with your subconscious. Your mind can just wander off or you think, 'Well, maybe I'll do it later,' and you never get back to it. This often is your subconscious wishing to hold onto old beliefs that it feels are protecting you, but actually it is the opposite – those very beliefs are hindering you. Your poor subconscious doesn't know the trauma is over. A practitioner can help to keep you on track throughout the session and when it's time to reimprint your new picture, they can gently guide you through the process. It is often nice for you to share your new picture of peace, calm or whatever you have recreated, with your practitioner to really reinforce it.

A qualified practitioner local to you can be found from the directory on the following website: www.matrixreimprinting.com You can view their individual profiles and contact them to see if it feels right to work with them. Most practitioners are happy to work online, so they don't have to be local to you. Many will offer a free consultation, to help you decide whether he/she is the right practitioner for you. It is imperative that you choose a practitioner you feel comfortable with, as this is a difficult time for you and you need to feel supported. Please go with your instinct.

A sceptic's experience

Jeremy had lost his forty-year-old daughter to cancer, and whilst a little unsure of Matrix Reimprinting, he decided to give it a try after speaking to several of his family members who had been to see me for various reasons. He had seen such a positive change in them that he thought it was worth giving it a go. He became very upset when he spoke about his daughter, and in particular her passing in hospital. He felt that she was uncomfortable as she passed over, and this was really playing on his mind. So, we began by tapping on his emotions, and when he felt a bit calmer, we went into the matrix and tapped on his ECHO, who was also very upset. After a few rounds of me tapping on him, and him tapping on his ECHO, he said that his ECHO was feeling a little better. Then, moving within the picture, he put some extra pillows under his daughter's head, and changed the décor in the room, to make it brighter and more comfortable for her. He then felt ready to have a private conversation with her higher self and they talked.

Afterwards, he tapped on the ECHOs of his other two daughters who had also been in the hospital room, and continued to tap until they were feeling calmer. When he felt satisfied that he had accomplished everything that needed to be done in the picture, those ECHOs also said goodbye to their sister. He then allowed the picture to play out with her passing peacefully. In his mind, she was helped across by some family members who had already passed away. He took the picture of her calm – almost angelic – peaceful passing, enveloped in a beautiful colour, into his heart, and his entire being was imbued with a positive new vision, which he then blasted out into the matrix.

Even though he was quite sceptical of basic energy techniques, let alone Matrix Reimprinting, he gave it a go, and was able to deal with the trauma and emotional pain of the loss of his daughter. Additionally, he helped clear some of the emotional pain for his other daughters, who both, incidentally, on separate occasions not long after this session, mentioned to him they felt more at peace with their feelings of loss. This in turn helped him to deal with his feelings regarding their loss, which had also weighed heavily on his heart. He talked afterwards about how he felt totally different about that fateful day and did compliment the Matrix Reimprinting process for helping him.

A splash of research

I will finish this chapter with a splash of research, for those of you who like that sort of thing. Feel free to skip this bit if it's not for you.

There is recent research ('Retrieval-induced plasticity is ideally placed to enable memories to be updated with new information') that supports the idea that memories are malleable and that when we retrieve these malleable memories, we can update them with new information.[1] With Matrix Reimprinting, that is exactly what we are doing: going into memories, clearing the shock, finding beliefs, and altering the memory.

Karim Nader, professor and researcher at McGill University, Montreal, Canada, has conducted extensive research on how fearful and traumatic memories are stored in the brain and how they can be manipulated. His work on rats has clearly demonstrated that it is possible to erase fearful memories using specific chemicals in the hope of developing medications.[2] Previously, it was believed that once memories are hardwired in your brain they stay there. This has now been shown not to be the case. Professor Nader and his team have discovered that memories, when recalled, can become unwired, thereby allowing for a window of opportunity to alter the memory. These researchers demonstrated that the neuronal circuits connecting the hippocampus let the amygdala know about sensory information (e.g. something upsetting has happened), after which the amygdala stamps the memory as emotionally significant and stores it for future use – to identify similar problems that could trigger a similar response. Are memories stored in the brain or out in the matrix? This can be the subject of a debate; I believe the latter to be true. If the memory is in the matrix, perhaps this is an ECHO, and when the trauma is cleared this ECHO can be fully integrated. We will no longer need to store these negative experiences for future reference – we will be able to transform our memories into more positive pictures that can instead be used to bring us peace and hopefully joy.

One pilot study specifically related to Matrix Reimprinting with 24 participants researched the effectiveness of this technique in a public health setting. It showed significant improvements in five different health measures of emotional wellbeing as well as a reduction in anxiety measurements.[3]

The benefits of using Matrix Reimprinting

- It can deal with the shock of grief.
- It can reduce emotional pain.
- It can take the intensity out of troubling memories.
- It can help relieve suffering, and quite frankly it can help to shift a lifetime of grieving heaviness.
- It can help resolve the unresolvable by changing key aspects of haunting memories.
- It can help to raise your vibration – maybe a little, maybe a lot – which in turn will help you feel better.
- It enables you to understand how specific negative beliefs may have shaped your life and change them to more positive supporting beliefs.
- It allows for a space to connect to your deceased loved ones.
- The Reimprinting process is gentle and transformative.

Joy Beyond Grief – Self-Love Exercises

If you decide to take my advice and seek a Matrix Reimprinting practitioner to work with, then by answering the following questions, you will have a clear idea of what you want to work on.

As you answer these questions, don't get too bogged down in details, as I do not want you to go straight into the memory, where you could potentially become upset. If you do find that you become upset at any point, please stop and do some tapping, as described in the previous chapter. Simply tap on how that memory is making you feel. If you get *very* upset, use the tap and distract technique I mentioned earlier. You could think about what you are having for dinner, or count the number of items in your room which begin with a certain letter, or you could even get out into nature for a while as a means of distraction. Another option could be the muscle relaxation exercise from chapter 3. Whatever you choose to do, just keep tapping, and then come back to the rest of the questions another time.

1/ Was there a shock involved in your loss? If so, when was it?

2/ Are there any specific times when you are particularly susceptible to thinking about your loss over and over again?

3/ Is there anything about your loss that you feel guilty about?

4/ Is there anything you regret saying or doing around the time of your loss?

5/ Are you angry about something that happened around the time of your loss?

6/ Is there something you just keep playing over and over in your mind?

7/ Has anyone said anything upsetting to you regarding your loss?

8/ Are there any feelings that something was left unresolved?

9/ Was there anything about the passing of your loved one that was not peaceful? (If their passing was violent, please just be aware this will probably need to be looked at with a practitioner.)

10/ Are there any specific memories you find upsetting?

Answers to the questions above will give you insight into what to work on with a practitioner. I would also recommend revisiting the questions at the end of chapter 4, as they will provide further insight. If you realise that you have been suffering for a long time, or are having trouble letting go, your answers to these would benefit from being looked at with a practitioner, too. In fact, the emotions that you wrote down on your *Healing Heart* can also be used as a starting point, as often there is a particular memory behind each of them.

Below is a practice exercise for you to try on your own.

A healing space to talk to your loved one

Before you begin the exercise, I would like to make it perfectly clear that this is not Matrix Reimprinting. It is merely another gentle, simple step for you to take on your healing journey.

This exercise is best done in the presence of your grief buddy, as they can offer support, and also tap with you if it all gets too emotional.

This exercise may not be for everyone, and you should only try it if you feel comfortable with its aims. Having said that, the benefits of doing this exercise have been well documented. Please see the *Resources* section for more information. It can certainly help you to feel better and gain some inner peace.

Find a peaceful, quiet space where you will not be disturbed for at least 15 minutes. You can either lie down or sit in a comfortable chair. Make sure you are warm enough, and have a drink of water to hand. Spend a moment allowing your body to relax – maybe do a couple of heart breaths to allow your body to calm down. Now, imagine you are in a place where you feel totally safe and relaxed. This can be a real place or somewhere imaginary. Take a moment to just be there.

When you feel comfortable, invite the higher self of your deceased loved one to join you. Just imagine them there with you. (This will be a different experience for everyone, so it is about you learning your own language of communication.) Take your time and be patient. As you clear shock from your system (using tapping and Matrix Reimprinting techniques), this exercise will become easier.

Just begin by saying a few words to them. The first time you do this, try not to get into anything which is very difficult for you. Simply express your feelings to them, and see if you receive anything back. You may or you may not. Either way, just allow whatever the experience brings to simply be. This is really about you being able to say whatever it is that you want to say to them. This can be a very enlightening and resolving process.

If you feel you are getting very emotional, just come out of the space, open your eyes, and tap, tap, tap. Keep tapping. Use the tap and distract technique until the emotion subsides. Focus on your heart breath and have a chat with your grief buddy.

I recommend that you write down your experience in your journal: what happened, how it felt, if you sensed that you received a response from your loved one – simply write down anything and everything that you believe to be important.

Chapter 8

BELIEFS, SPIRITUALITY, AND THE SOUL

'Honouring the world of form and spirit;
surrendering to endless death and rebirth;
this is the source of all healing.'
Theodore Tsaousidis

I RECALL THAT AFTER MY father's death, I experienced a profound fear of God. Should I be trying to talk to this God to ensure that my father was OK, I asked myself. I also remember wondering if I had done something wrong, and that's why my dad had been taken away from me. If God could do this, what other horrendous things was He/She capable of? These thoughts, as well as the deeper feelings that they provoked, are still clear in my mind to this day. I was brought up in a vaguely Christian environment, but I only remember going to church for weddings and funerals, and personally, I always found churches and what was being said in them to be very harsh, unloving, and a bit scary.

After my fear of God subsided, I became angry. Boy oh boy was I angry. How could a so-called kind, life-giving God do this? My childhood, which had been filled with laughter, fun, exploration, and unequivocal optimism, all came to an abrupt end when my dad died. I was so angry that I totally turned my back on any God. For many, many years, even the mention of God in any form, or within any religious context, would make my blood boil.

Gradually, over the course of my life, and as a result of the losses I have experienced and the subsequent healing journey I have sought, I have come to a place of spiritual contentment. Not only can I now mention the word 'God', but I am happy to use it interchangeably with creator, source, and higher intelligence, to name but a few. This all sits very comfortably with me now. It explains a lot about life and death, and is part of my journey from fear to love and peace. My belief, for today at least, is that we are a soul having a human experience. I am in total agreement with Wayne Dyer who said, 'Begin to see yourself as a soul with a body rather than a body with a soul.'[1] By thinking of ourselves as a soul, having a human experience, we become free to discover the full range of what it means to be human. While this obviously has its wonderful highs, in grief and loss it has its harsh challenges.

Obviously, I am not expecting your journey to include, as mine has, a change in your fundamental beliefs: your journey will always be individual to you. However, recall from the last chapter how your beliefs become your reality, and consider that maybe it's a good idea to have a closer look at them. By helping yourself to heal, you may deepen an already strong belief in, say, a specific religious faith. Or, the journey may bring up some old beliefs that you thought you had left behind a long time ago, but that now seem to make sense again. Also, by looking at your beliefs, you may help restore a feeling of connection with a loved one who has passed.

Shifts in beliefs

'Most of my patients discover that the major changes in their views of God or a higher power related to times in their lives when a major change or loss occurred,' writes Paul Pearsall in his book *Super Joy*.[2] This was certainly true for me, and has been for many of my clients too. Loss is often a powerful catalyst for deeper introspection and questioning of the nature of existence and our belief systems, and specifically, what happens following death. It has become apparent to me that there are clear patterns that emerge when looking at those who have come to peace with their loss through gentle, supporting spiritual beliefs and those who have struggled for many years with their grief and feel bitterness, anger, and resentment towards death.

Having worked with so many clients, one particular thing stands out. When people work through their pain, whatever their beliefs were before their loss, they almost always come to a gentle, kind, and loving understanding of the world and their part in it. This in turn appears to lead the way for them to reconnect to those loved ones who have passed, and then, very interestingly, magical things begin to happen. I have had clients who have *smelled* their loved one's aroma; clients who, whenever they needed help in life, became aware of a comment their loved one had made when they were alive that helped them. (I could go on and on.)

When I was fearful of God, I was fearful of living. When I was angry with God, I was angry with life along with everyone and everything in it. Remember, our beliefs become our reality, so clearing out whatever was lingering behind those feelings enabled me to change my beliefs. I was able to arrive at a place of peace that made total sense to me and is now a fully integrated part of me. I now regard myself as a spiritual person. I am a soul having a human experience, and what an experience! As I clear away layers of learnt issues (well, the unhelpful ones at least), I get nearer and nearer to my true self, and closer and closer to understanding my soul journey.

For me, death is a transition from our human experience back into soul. I believe my father, my husband, and numerous family members who have passed have simply shed their human self, much like a butterfly sheds its cocoon or as a snake sheds its skin. Saint Augustine said, 'The dead are invisible, they are not absent.'[3] Françoise Dolto stated, 'The invisible are present and around us and they guide us.'[4] These words echo what I have come to believe after working through my own grieving experience. It is about learning to move through the pain and to experience the language of love beyond the death veil. Your own experience will be individual and specific for you, but remember how I am always seeing buzzards? They are part of my language of love.

What do you believe, and how does it affect the language of love that you share with your lost loved one? Big questions. Take time to mull them over, and if it feels right, make some notes in your journal. Do you still feel your own personal love connection with the one you love? Please don't feel bad if you don't; it will happen when the pain subsides, and the love flows through. Always keep a lookout for those synchronicities that speak to your connection, and be ready to enjoy those special moments when they present themselves.

You may feel as though you just don't know what to believe in, but rest assured: that is a very familiar feeling for many people. The good news is that you can always utilise EFT no matter where you are, so you always have a starting point. You can tap on 'I just don't know what to believe in,' or 'I'm just hurting so much that I don't know what to think.' Whatever you are feeling, tap on it. Information related to those statements may surface while you're tapping, as the feelings that they represent are actually guiding you through shifting whatever it is that needs clearing. So do get tapping. However, bear in mind that if you are recently bereaved, this may take some time. It would be best to follow the advice offered in the early chapters first, such as to just tap on immediate feelings, and not to worry about your beliefs until you feel ready to confront them. Always do what feels right for you.

Death and a kitten

Let's take a more in-depth look at beliefs surrounding death, and what may happen to you when you die. If you were brought up in the Western hemisphere, death and dying is almost a taboo subject. It has become a very scary aspect of life, and society in general seems to go to great lengths to keep the majority of us away from looking at death, much less talking about it. My experience was a classic example of this. Less than an hour after my dad died, my mum sent my brother and me to buy a kitten while they took my father's body out of the house to the funeral parlour. *A kitten!!!* Don't get me wrong, I love kittens, but less than an hour after my dad had died was not the most appropriate time to bring a new pet into the home. My mum just could not bear to allow my brother and me to see my dead dad. I would have liked to have seen him but it was just not the *done thing*.

Another example of how we try to hide and ignore death, or its imminent arrival, is how we treat our elderly. We place them in homes, often far away from friends and loved ones. This is not a criticism, but rather an observation. Everybody is just so busy now, with people working longer hours just to make ends meet, that we no longer have the time or resources to care for our elderly in a loving family environment. This is also not a criticism of care homes. I have had direct experience with a few of them, and the effort put in by the staff is exemplary in the majority of cases. Rather, it is just another case of how we distance ourselves from death's onset and how it is such a taboo subject.

Is death the end or not?

Considering the prevailing Newtonian view of the body, it hardly comes as a surprise that Western medicine sees all of our organs as mechanical in nature, with the brain being in total control. Thus, when the brain is dead, that's it – the end. The end of any form of consciousness, and with it any talk of spiritual matters, soul transitioning, or continuing life force energy. Conversely, these spiritual concepts are prevalent in Eastern traditions and among many of the indigenous populations around the world. So, at one end of the spectrum there is the view that when you are dead, that's it, while at the other end, the belief is that we are simply a soul which reincarnates through several bodies, possibly over multiple centuries. And then, there are any number of social, cultural, and religious views falling somewhere in between.

So, what are your views on death, and more importantly, how are they impacting your own grieving experience? If you have been brought up in the West, this may seem a difficult question, as talking about death may not be a familiar topic of conversation for you. In fact, I'm sure that if you hadn't experienced your loss, it probably wouldn't be a talking point for you now. (If this is you, please tap as you are reading to allow your body to gently hear these words.) Alternatively, you might have experienced previous losses, and now, your latest loss is making you revisit those old feelings again, as you question what death actually is. Remember you have your grief buddy, so if it feels right to do so, have that conversation with them – and don't forget to tap while you talk.

Do you believe that when you're dead, you're dead and that's it? Maybe you have religious views that are giving you comfort at this time of loss. Maybe you have always been an atheist, and your loss is about coming to terms with this absolute finality. Maybe you believed in some form of God or spiritual being, which is comforting you, or you are feeling as I did – just so angry with Him/Her for allowing this to happen. Maybe everything is just too difficult to make sense of at this moment. All of these views, and hundreds more, have been experienced by millions of people for centuries. I invite you to spend time writing about your own beliefs on death in your journal and talking about them to your grief buddy. You can do your heart breathing before and after and be kind and gentle with yourself whilst doing this.

Spend time understanding your own beliefs. It will be helpful for two main reasons. Firstly, your beliefs about death will certainly be impacting how you are coping at this moment, and if those beliefs are not acting in your best interests in terms of your grieving, we'll work together to help them work for you. Secondly, beliefs have such a profound effect on you in all aspects of your life. And here, I'm going to say what I have said before, but in slightly different words: 'Your beliefs create your reality.' Therefore, addressing your beliefs about loss will have much wider implications for you in life as a whole. Maybe it is appropriate to look into this now or maybe it's too soon. Remember, only do what feels right for you.

Beliefs before loss

We have looked at beliefs surrounding what happens after death, and our beliefs of who we really are. Here, I would like to spend a little time exploring other beliefs we may hold. As discussed in previous chapters, throughout our lives and particularly during childhood, events, traumas, and shocks occur that cause us to form all sorts of beliefs. What we come into grief with is a whole set of pre-existing notions. These beliefs have an impact on our grieving process, which is why it bears repeating that, by looking at or uncovering them, we can truly begin to transform our lives, and not just deal with our loss. Loss can be a catalyst for change if desired.

From my experience, beliefs that you come into grief with can be traced using Matrix Reimprinting. By asking one ECHO to show another related memory, you can find your way back to where a particular belief first took root. Are you aware of any events in your life that seem to have a repeating pattern or theme to them? Have a think. Some are obvious, but more often than not, we don't see the connections because they are stored in our subconscious. Here is an example to clarify this.

Frances

I worked with Frances who had lost a brother when she was young. She had also experienced some unkindness from her father. She came to me because she was so upset about her son leaving home under unhappy circumstances. We did some Matrix work on the last time she saw her son, and we cleared some upset from the ECHO of that memory – particularly the loss and separation aspect. We then asked the ECHO if there were any other memories that it wanted to show us. Another memory came up, which on the surface seemed unrelated, but as we worked on it together, all soon became clear.

The second memory was about how Frances had felt somehow separate from a social group which she belonged to. The memory was about an incident where she felt they had left her out of an event which she thought she was going to be a part of. We cleared the upset here, which was about feeling separate from the friends she had become close to. We also worked with a third memory in which separation was the theme – she had not consciously been aware of the connections at all.

Finally, an ECHO showed her a memory from a time before her brother died. She was having dinner with her family, and her father said, 'You will never be as good as your brother. I don't even really see you as part of this family.' That was it – that one statement heard as a child was enough for my client to form the belief: 'I don't feel good enough to be with loved ones or people I care about.' Her subconscious went about keeping her separate from loved ones, and people and things that she cared about. This was amplified when she lost her brother, because for her it confirmed her feelings of separation. That belief had played out so many times in her life, and when she realised this and cleared that belief and all the pain connected to it, everything changed. Her life transformed. Beliefs like Frances' are known as limiting beliefs, as they quite literally limit your life.

Believe me, that was not an exceptional client experience – it is the norm. Clients often discover old beliefs that are not working for them anymore, and after clearing that trapped energy, they then go on to live a far happier and more contented life. With that in mind, please be aware of how powerful beliefs can be. If it is a good, inspiring belief, that's brilliant – keep playing it out in your life. However, if something other than your loss has been troubling you in your life, then behind it is probably a thread going back to some point where you formed a belief from a life experience, and I can bet your bottom dollar that that same thread will be playing some role in your loss. Your loss can be an access point to that thread. This is another reason why I asked you to fill in the *Healing Heart* as those emotions you wrote down may well play a role in an early-formed belief which is playing some part in your loss.

In the aforementioned book *Transform Your Beliefs, Transform Your Life*, the authors explain how our deep-rooted beliefs have much more of an influence on us than we often realise. As the title of the book indicates, by transforming your beliefs you can transform your life. My aim here is not to try and convince you to change your beliefs – I am simply inviting you to acknowledge where your beliefs lie in regard to death. If they are helping you at this difficult time, that's good. However, if your beliefs are adding to your pain, maybe they can be moved around to help and support you instead of adding to your problems. Old, outdated beliefs that do not serve you can be changed to help you on your healing journey. You really can clear those old limiting beliefs, and I cannot overstate how doing this can have a profound and positive impact on your life. Dreams can come true, and people can find themselves in jobs, situations, and places that they thought were beyond them. I invite you to be open, and to keep working through all the previous self-love exercises to help you through your grief. You will know when the time is right to explore further, should you wish to do so.

Death and spirituality

What does spirituality even mean? This term can be interpreted in many different ways, but here I refer to spirituality as an inner path to truth and knowing, involving the human spirit and soul. Incidentally, you do not have to be religious to be spiritual. Spirituality may sound very attractive, and will already be something that you feel is part of you. Or it may all sound a bit too fluffy. Either way, let's have a look at what some have described as spiritual experiences.

The first of these concepts is that of near-death experiences (NDE). There are quite literally hundreds of reports of such incidents, with many of them coming from highly respected psychiatrists, neuroscientists, and cardiologists.

Michael Sabom, MD has written extensively on NDEs. In his book *Light and Death*, he explains that originally he didn't think NDEs could provide any insight into life after death. However, with the advancement in medical procedures that now allow doctors to bring people back from what would have previously been defined as death, he has changed his mind on the matter. People regularly report experiencing moving towards a bright light, feelings of total peace, and indescribable, unconditional love. Some recall meeting deceased loved ones, and claim that they did not want to return to their conscious human state. Individuals who have had these experiences come back to life with a new perspective, which often includes the fact that they no longer fear death. This topic is far too vast to cover in detail here, but for more information on how people's lives have been transformed by NDEs, please refer to Michael Sabom's book, any of Dr Brian Weiss's excellent works or Anita Moorjani's book *Dying to be Me*. I believe that these documented experiences will give you some reassurance, hope, and peace regarding your deceased loved ones.

In contemplating death, it is common for our own mortality to come to the forefront. If this provokes fear in you, it is something worth addressing, because that is a clear indication that your body is stressed, and therefore your whole being is stressed. This fear of death can often come from shock, such as the shock of loss in grief, which in turn can develop into a belief, such as 'The world is a dangerous place'. Although it may feel that you can't transform that fear because it feels so huge, I want to assure you that you can. Tapping on that fear will help to clarify and ultimately clear what is behind it, making it possible to invite more love and peace into your life. Any love connections, let alone any form of spirituality, will be very difficult to experience if you are trapped in fear. Fear is at one end of a spectrum, and love at the other. You can't be in both at the same time. If you are in fear, you are in protection/survival mode, and if you are in love, you are in growth mode. Use tapping to move away from fear and towards love. If you feel any of this resonates with you, and the fear is sometimes overwhelming you, please use tapping and discuss this with an EFT or Matrix Reimprinting practitioner.

One's soul

The question of what the soul is, and whether or not we even have one, is a subject which has long been discussed. Do we have to be spiritual to have one? What is its purpose? While these can be highly charged questions, one thing is for sure – these conversations have been going on forever. Pythagoras spoke extensively on the subject of the soul, believing not only that humans have souls, but animals and plants do too. Socrates wrote about the soul being immortal, while Aristotle said that to live happily is an inward power of the soul.

> 'You have to grow from the inside out. None
> can reach you, none can make you spiritual.
> There is no other teacher than your soul.'
> Swami Vivekananda

This quote really emphasises the fact that growth always comes from within, and that your soul leads the way. You are the only one who can heal you. Your soul is the part of you that is your truth, the part of you that gets the bigger picture of why you are here – it is the all-knowing you. Believe it or not, your soul has all the answers you will ever need. Others can guide you and help you along your journey, much as I aim to do with this book, but ultimately the only one who can heal or change you *is* you. That is why it is so important to do the self-love exercises at the end of each chapter – so that you can truly begin to experience the healing and change.

What do <u>you</u> think or feel? If it feels right and loving, that's what it is. If it feels uncomfortable or upsetting, use the tools in this book to transform those feelings and thoughts, so that you can be clear about what you <u>do</u> believe.

And as you work through the book and the self-love exercises, I invite you to view yourself, your deceased loved ones – in fact, everyone you know – as a soul having a human experience. I invite you to see souls as all-knowing and pure in intention. I invite you to feel, or at least try to feel, at peace with your loved one's transition. I invite you to see that transition as having gone back to pure soul, where they are fine – more than fine even. They get it. They get it all. It's us that do not always get it. How can we understand these great universal truths from our narrow human perspective? We can't be expected to. However, seeing their passing as a transition can change everything. Remember the beautiful stories of those who have gone through NDEs. According to those people, as well as many writings on this topic, being in true soul form is true bliss.

When you have experienced incredible pain such as in loss, that pain can either act as a barrier or a source of potential. Viewing ourselves as a soul in human form, and understanding our life as only a small part of our soul's journey, can be so helpful to us – not only in terms of giving meaning to our existence, and specifically to the pain we go through with grief, but as a means for recognising the potential for transformation. It can be magical if we see with different eyes and open ourselves up to celebrate the next stage of our journey: a journey of pure love. Then we, too, can grow and expand, having true fun and creating joy for ourselves in this lifetime, until reunited in soul form with our deceased loved ones.

The soul has a function while we are in human form, and that is to guide us. Christiane Northrup puts it succinctly in her wonderful book *Making Life Easy: A Simple Guide to a Divinely Inspired Life*. When speaking of the soul, she says, 'The soul is a force that is far greater than intellect. Call it inner guidance, call it a hunch or a feeling that results in goose bumps – whatever you call it, your job is to call upon it for assistance and guidance.'[4] This is the part of you to call upon in times of need. It is always there – we just need to understand how to hear it. With your soul being so intimately intertwined with your heart, I invite you to listen hard to your heart, not your intellect (brain). Your brain is there to implement what your heart knows or decides. I invite you to listen to your heart, which will only ever be gentle and loving.

I believe that the heart is the bridge to the soul. It has long been apparent to me that the more clients clear in terms of fear, pain, and unhelpful beliefs, the better they are able to recognise their own inner truth and love. In turn, the better they are able to access the connection to their loved ones who have passed. The beauty of this shows itself in such individual and inspiring ways through the language of love. You, too, can experience this for yourself. Just gently follow the exercises in the book at your own pace.

I finish this chapter with a message from Joan, a client, writing about her husband:

'Yesterday, on the actual anniversary of Liam's death, a single red rosebud came out on the rose bush planted with love in Liam's memory in our front garden! I believe it is a sign from you, my love. In December, a rose coming out?? Thank you darling, for all your help from the other side.' Joan was so comforted by this – it was her language of love, bridging that separation between life and death. When we really listen to our heart, it will not deceive us!

Now, let us explore further your own beliefs around loss, what happens after death, what spirituality means to you, and your thoughts on the soul. Below are several questions for you to consider if the time feels right for you to do so. If it does feel right, go ahead and answer with as much honesty and love towards yourself as possible. Take your time, ponder and explore, or even better, discuss what you discover with your grief buddy. If it doesn't feel right at this moment in time, come back to these questions when it does.

Joy Beyond Grief – Self-Love Exercise

Start by putting some time aside for the exercise. Sit comfortably with a drink of water to hand, and begin by doing your heart breathing. Use your journal to write down your answers.

Stop at any point you feel upset, and tap on what that emotion is. For example, if your answer to number 1 is *I don't believe there is anything after death* and it makes you feel sad, you can tap on 'Even though I feel sad as I don't believe there is anything after death, I'm OK' or say 'I'm here' if saying 'I'm OK' is too much for you. If the emotion feels too strong to deal with on your own, then work through these questions with a practitioner. As in the self-love exercise in the previous chapter, remember that if you get very upset, KEEP TAPPING and start thinking about something different, such as what you are having for dinner, or count the number of items in your room which begin with a certain letter or take yourself out in nature for a while – but keep tapping until you feel better. In this case I urge you to speak to a practitioner. You could instead do the muscle relaxation exercise from chapter 3 and come back to the rest of the questions another time.

1/ What are your beliefs about the following statement: 'Death is the end, there is nothing after at all.'

2/ Are you aware of any beliefs you have developed from previous losses? Or, are you aware of any beliefs resulting from this present loss? (Generally, these are subconscious.)

3/ Do you believe that you can change your beliefs?

4/ Would you like to change any beliefs you have about death?

5/ Does the thought of your own death cause you to feel fear?

6/ Do you believe that you have a soul? If so, what does that mean to you?

7/ What are your beliefs on spirituality?

If you have a strong belief that you do not feel was mentioned above, then please add it to your journal. Once you have made some notes on the questions above, separate them into ones which feel comforting and empowering and those which don't.

The empowering, positive, and supportive beliefs you hold about your spirituality, around matters of the soul or indeed, death itself, may include 'I believe my deceased loved one is back in soul and at peace', or 'I believe the soul of my departed loved one and my own soul will always be connected through love'. Whatever the form they take, you could do one of the following to reinforce them and to help reassure yourself.

1/ Write them out on Post-it notes and place them around the house.

2/ Draw or paint a beautiful picture around the words.

3/ Draw or paint a picture that represents these beliefs to you.

4/ Knit, sew or crochet them onto something.

5/ Record yourself saying them, then play them back to yourself in the bath, when you wake up or are going to sleep.

6/ Have them put on a piece of jewellery.

7/ Carve them into metal or wood.

8/ Have them as your wallpaper on your computer and/or phone so you see them regularly.

9/ Write a poem incorporating them in it.

10/ Have a special place in your garden or somewhere in nature that you associate with these beliefs so that when you go there, it reminds you of them.

By using your creativity with these beliefs, you will be steadily reminding yourself of them and reinforcing them, and you will, in turn, help to raise your vibration.

For those beliefs which are uncomfortable, and disempowering to you, it is a good idea to use tapping. You may have already done this whilst writing them down, but if you haven't, then please tap on how those beliefs are making you feel. Take your time to work through each of them. As previously said, it may be advisable to work with your EFT or Matrix Reimprinting practitioner, as these beliefs may be deep-rooted and may well benefit from additional help. By finding the source of your beliefs, you are often able to make changes to them that you just can't in the space you are in now. I have seen many clients with extremely disempowering beliefs who, with Matrix Reimprinting, found where those beliefs came from, saw them in a different light, and could transform them to be a support – not a hindrance – in their lives. This can happen for you too.

Chapter 9

GRIEF AND PHYSICAL WELLBEING

'Sometimes it's OK if the only thing
you did today was breathe.'
Yumi Sakugawa

GRIEF AFFECTS EVERY ASPECT OF our being – emotional, energetic, psychological, spiritual, and physical. In previous chapters, we have looked at how the body functions energetically, and the role of emotions in grief. We have explored how our psychology, spirituality, and the soul affect and are affected by loss. In this chapter, we will address how grief can have a profound negative effect on your physical body.

You may be thinking that you have gone through enough as it is without being frightened by the possibility of becoming physically unwell, and obviously it is not my intention to scare you. However, it is important for you to know the realities of what could happen to your physical body if you choose to join the Keep Yourself Busy Brigade, suppressing your feelings and ignoring your emotions. This chapter is included to help you understand the connection between your physical body, your mind, and your experience of loss.

What I am talking about here is being responsible for what is happening to you, which means being aware, using all the necessary self-help tools and techniques recommended, and seeking practitioners recommended in this book if necessary. They are all here to help you with whatever area of grief you need help to deal with. This chapter is all about knowledge, prevention, and empowerment. The more knowledge you have, the easier it will be to prevent further problems, thus empowering you while you are grieving. Whether you have experienced some physical problems or not, this chapter will help you understand the mind-body connection and its relationship to grief.

If we are to believe that you are a soul having the human experience *life*, I'm sure you will agree that your physical body is rather crucial. In fact, it's a rather crucial part of you even if you don't believe that! Your physical body is who you identify with in this life. And maybe, just maybe, any physical problems you encounter in your life are not just random acts of your body malfunctioning. Maybe physical problems are part of a complex system which, if left uncared for, sees them as part of a solution to unresolved emotional issues, and particularly shocks such as grief. This certainly is the belief of many now and is fundamental to that new health paradigm which includes META-Health and the next generation of this model: META Consciousness, developed by Penny Croal (both of which you can find out more about in the *Resources* section at the end of the book).

More about META Consciousness

META Consciousness is founded on the biological, psychological and social connections within each of us and focuses on illnesses and physical conditions and their individual meanings to you. It is not a therapy, but rather a way to assess what is happening to your body during illness or a health condition of either the mental or physical variety. It incorporates connections between organs of the body, stress, emotions, beliefs, and phases of healing. It works on the premise that your body never makes a mistake. This begs the question of what is going on when you become ill, or you are experiencing some physical pain or medical condition. When your body has experienced a shock of some kind, such as a loss, it has the potential to manifest the loss as a physical problem if left unchecked. Basically, your body is just shouting louder, to make you listen and do something about it. Undealt-with shock can have a huge impact on your physical health, and how you interpret it may elicit different health conditions. I will come back to this in a while.

The META Consciousness approach to health is growing in prominence, as some medical doctors are now actively engaging with it. It is a truly holistic approach to healing. I haven't got the space in this book to go into it as deeply as I would like, as it is relatively complex. If this is something you are particularly interested in, please see the *Resources* section. Here, I will discuss its relevance to loss.

As I mentioned earlier, if you research causes of illness in medical books, you will find that 95 per cent of all illnesses fall into the category *Unknown Cause*. According to Bruce Lipton, 95 per cent of all illnesses are due to stress and 100 per cent of stress is due to your perception. He is famous for his saying, 'It's the environment, stupid,' implying that what is happening in your environment is having a massive impact on your health and wellbeing. If you have just lost a loved one, then your environment can be a very stressful place. Bruce includes in the word 'environment' the environment of your cells within your body; your body can be a stressful place for your cells with the shock of loss affecting them. If shock is not dealt with, then you move into suffering either emotionally or physically. META Consciousness helps you to find the cause of the different illnesses, diseases, and conditions which have possibly occurred due to the stress, the shock, or the specific beliefs around losing a loved one.

Rare physical problems associated with grief

Let's now look at a few physical health issues associated with grief that, while rare, are worthy of a mention, because if they are affecting you, this information may go some way towards helping you. Firstly, there are chest pains. These can show up as pressure in the chest, sharp pains, aching in the chest (heart) area, irregular heartbeats, or a heavy feeling. Although no one can say exactly why you can experience these symptoms, the Imperial College London suggests it may be the heart's way of protecting itself from the surge of adrenaline, which occurs due to the shock of grief. Heart palpitations and pain in the chest area have been given the title 'Broken Heart Syndrome', also known by the more technical terms 'Stress-induced Cardiomyopathy' or 'Takotsubo Cardiomyopathy'. Symptoms can mimic a heart attack, but there are some fundamental differences. Blood tests show no damage to the heart, tests show no blockage in the coronary arteries, and EKG results do not look the same as for those who have experienced a heart attack. It is said to be brought on by a surge in flight or fight hormones, and can be very frightening. These symptoms normally occur closely following the loss of someone and are generally gone within a few days to a week.[1] As I said, this is uncommon, but if this is affecting you in any way, then take a visit to your doctor for professional advice. Obviously, this goes for any and all physical health problems you may be experiencing. Get along to your doctor. Ask your grief buddy to go with you for support.

Some common physical problems associated with grief

It is quite common that some form of anxiety-based feelings recognised by the British Psychological Society come with grief. These include shaking, churning stomach, fast heart rate, sweating, headaches, and hypersensitivity. These symptoms can last from a few days to much longer if you do not work through the emotional pain of grief. General aches and pains are not uncommon either. People describe sore or aching muscles and joints. Studies show that for up to twelve months after the loss of a husband, widows can experience an increase of 56.3 per cent of physical pain in a sample study of 1,000 people.[2] This was related to their mood disturbances due to their bereavement. Again, this is not to frighten you, but rather to let you know that, if this is happening to you, it is commonplace. EFT is well documented for its help with physical pain, so please use it to help yourself to feel better.

META Consciousness's understanding of grief

My daughter had vitiligo – a skin condition where there is a problem with the pigmentation. She had several discoloured patches of skin on her stomach area and although it was not painful in any way, it made her feel very self-conscious. She had had it for a while, but it wasn't until I learnt about META-Health and subsequently META Consciousness that I realised it was related to a shock to her body in which a brutal separation stressor had occurred. It then became obvious that her vitiligo had developed after her father had died, and these two issues were connected. With this realisation, we were able to do the necessary energy work, and her vitiligo completely disappeared and has not come back since. With the skin being the largest organ of the body, it is no surprise that it can be affected by grief. In META Consciousness terms, if you perceive your loss as a brutal separation, then there can be a potential for a skin problem.

Different shocks may elicit different health conditions in a similar area of the body. Another skin problem associated with separation is eczema. Things can get a bit more complex than this, because different skin layers such as the epidermis, dermis and the hypodermis may all have slightly different meanings in terms of loss. If eczema is affecting you, please refer to the *Resources* section for further information.

From a META Consciousness perspective, there are other physical health problems commonly related to loss, such as testicular or ovarian problems and water retention, which are related to isolation and shocks caused by feelings of abandonment. Different parts of the body will be affected depending on how you personally perceived your loss. Loss is individual and while one person may feel a profound loss, another may be submerged in the feeling of separation from their loved one. Slight differences in personal perspective will be highly influential in the potential manifestation of any physical issues. So, please remember that dealing with the shock of loss reduces the potential for physical issues to arise.

Whilst the mainstream medical profession certainly acknowledges that loss can have a profound impact on your health, it doesn't make the deeper connections that META Consciousness does. These connections enable you to be very specific in dealing with the underlying shock (Remember from chapter 3 that META-Health term UDIN? It is a shock that was unexpected, dramatic, isolating or where the person experiencing it had no strategy to deal with it.) Connections between shocks, physical symptoms, and loss can make sense from the META Consciousness approach.

Katherine

Let me explain further. Katherine had recently lost her grandchild and was obviously in deep grief; she also developed some stomach problems soon after, with a tightening and knotting in her stomach, which was quite painful. She did feel that her loss and her stomach pains were related in some way, but did not understand the connection. As we tapped, she realised that she was holding onto her grief because she felt so guilty that she was alive and her grandchild was dead. (Often stomach issues are related to holding onto things.) We worked through the stuck energy of exactly what she was afraid to let go of and the guilt she was feeling, and not only did she feel much better, but her stomach problem went away completely. She then understood the connection between her loss and her stomach pains.

I'll finish with a couple of examples of how an understanding of META Consciousness can help with any physical issues related to grief.

Do you remember Deirdre who lost her baby brother when she was only a very young child, and who came to me in her late fifties? What I didn't mention was she came to me regarding her chronic lower back problem. Do you know what chronic lower back problems are related to according to META Consciousness? They are related to severe self-worth issues. How do you think Deirdre felt after being blamed for the death of her baby brother? Yes, you guessed it: severely low about herself. With Matrix Reimprinting, her feelings of self-worth improved as did her back to a large extent.

Ghislaine

Ghislaine came to me having suffered from chest pains for a long time, and although the doctors could not find anything mechanically wrong with her heart, she nevertheless had chest pains which would range in severity. Having worked through a few painful events in her life, we went back in one session to when her mother died. She was only a young teenager then, and was now in her mid-fifties. She realised in this session that she had never really had a chance to mourn her mother's death. After spending some time using EFT and Matrix Reimprinting, she settled in a place of peace, and her chest pains stopped completely. So again, be reassured these energy techniques are very powerful in helping you with physical issues.

As opposed to just dealing with symptoms, META Consciousness provides an informative way of viewing the body – a way to get to the core of a problem and the emotional and physical connections. With the right knowledge, you can use the appropriate techniques to clear what is behind the presenting physical problem and move your life forward to a less stressed physical state. Without physical problems, your grief healing journey will be a little lighter. META Consciousness as a concept is constantly evolving and even more wonderful understandings of how emotional traumas can affect physical health are developing.

Joy Beyond Grief – Self-Love Exercise

I invite you to think about any physical symptoms or conditions you are experiencing, and in particular any that have occurred since your loss. By addressing any physical problems, you will be working towards resolving them and you will also be seeing if there is a connection between them and your loss. You will be allowing yourself to understand how your physical body is expressing your own grieving experience. Write down your symptoms in your journal, including how much they are affecting your life. (If you are not experiencing any physical issues, please go on to the next section, 'Bringing in light and love'.)

You now have a point at which you can start to use EFT and Matrix Reimprinting to help yourself.

Step 1 - Decide which physical ailment you are going to work on. Or work on your choice with a practitioner if you prefer; this will help you on a deeper level.

Step 2 - Familiarise yourself again with the tapping sequence from chapter 6 if you need to, and/or watch the video of me tapping on the points.

Step 3 - Make sure you have a rating of intensity on a particular physical issue. It is important to note here that, at this moment, this physical issue may not be very intense at all, but for the purpose of getting going with using EFT for physical issues, try and tune in to when it has been intense.

Step 4 - Begin with tapping on the SH point whilst saying, 'Even though I have … (say your physical issue here), I am OK'. Repeat this 3 times. Then, going around the points, say your physical issue at each point. For example, 'These achy muscles' or 'This headache'. Tap about 7 times on each point.

Step 5 - Re-rate your original intensity. Is it the same, has it gone down, has it gone up or has something physical changed?

If it's gone down, that's great. Keep tapping to get it right down to zero if you can. If it's gone up, although rare, it can happen and is usually a sign that a deeper, more hidden, emotion is surfacing, so keep tapping. Remember, undealt-with emotions or shocks may show up as physical problems, so as you tap, the related emotion or shock may come up. If this happens, start tapping on the emotion instead, as this is getting closer to the source of the problem. As I've recommended in all the exercises, if you get overwhelmingly emotional, plan to work with a practitioner. In the moment though, tap and distract.

If it is a pain you are experiencing, and it seems to move around the body, this is quite normal in the EFT world. You should follow the pain, which is called 'chasing the pain'.

For example, if you start by tapping on a pain in your head and then the pain moves down into your neck, change your words to 'this pain in my neck' and if the pain moves again, keep changing the words. If an emotion comes up, that's good as you're getting closer to the issue itself rather than only the symptom of the problem, i.e. the physical pain. So proceed by tapping on the presenting emotion. But remember: if necessary, tap and distract and seek a practitioner.

Your aim is to keep tapping until you bring the pain down to an intensity of at least a 2 or 3. If you recognise a specific emotional feeling and are not able to bring the intensity down very far, or if a particular, disturbing memory comes up, then it is a good idea to make a note of what happened and work with your practitioner on the issue.

Talk to your grief buddy about any concerns you have and most importantly of all, visit your doctor for any and all physical problems you may be experiencing.

Bringing in light and love

This simple, gentle exercise provides a balance to the tapping work just completed. Sit or lie comfortably where you will not be disturbed for about

10 minutes. Make sure you are warm and have a drink of water to hand. Now, gently take your awareness to any part of your body where there is a health issue, condition, pain or ache. (If you are physically well, take your awareness to your heart area.) As you bring all your awareness to this area, take a moment to truly tune in to this place, and then imagine bringing light into this part of your body. Imagine bringing in a beautiful, healing white light. Imagine this light flooding the area of your body that you are focusing on. Have the intention that this white light is bringing in a true healing to your body and imagine in whichever way feels right for you that this light is working with your body to help heal it. Know this light is full of love and allow it time to do its thing. Send kindness to your body and thank it for showing you that something needs dealing with and keep that light flooding in. Let this part of your body know you are committed to helping it become healthy and radiant. Then, imagine that white light going through every area of your body. After a few minutes of allowing this to occur, and when it feels right, bring your awareness to your breathing and wiggle your fingers and toes. Then bring your awareness to the room you are in. When you are ready, open your eyes. Have some water and take your time to gently get up and go about your day.

Chapter 10

TRANSGENERATIONAL GRIEF AND LIFE PATTERNS

'What we call chaos is just patterns we
haven't recognised. What we call random
is just patterns we can't decipher.'
Chuck Palahniuk

VINCENT VAN GOGH IS KNOWN throughout the world for his paintings. It is not, however, widely known that he was born 30th March 1852, one year to the day after his older brother of the same name died. As well as being given his older brother's first name, he was also given his middle name, Wilhelm. His family was not willing to discuss the death of his older brother at all, and this appears to have had a massive impact on him. His life became quite tragic, as he felt as though he was 'forbidden to exist'.[1] Van Gogh even made a suicide attempt after receiving correspondence from his other brother Theo, carrying the news that he had named his own son Vincent, out of the love he had for him. As he read about his brother's hopes and dreams for the newborn baby, the artist was revisited by the feeling that he could not coexist with another living Vincent.

Other tragic events in van Gogh's life, such as the famous cutting-off of his own ear, and ultimately his tragic death by suicide, speaks to the pain that this man experienced throughout his life. This is such a poignant example of what can happen when a whole family cannot or does not grieve for a child. One can only speculate on what van Gogh's life might have been like if his brother's death had been spoken of, fully grieved, or dealt with from an energetic perspective. This is one of many examples of what is referred to in psychotherapy as a 'replacement child' – a child conceived to replace a recently deceased relative. They are often given the same name of the deceased child, and birthdays can correspond. Although I am not a fan of this term, it does describe one aspect of transgenerational grief in a very succinct way.

What is transgenerational grief

Transgenerational grief is grief which is passed down through the generations and is experienced by an individual in many forms, including emotional issues and physical or psychological problems. It can occur as a result of being a replacement child, or of what is known as 'historical unresolved grief'. This can take the form of individual trauma following a traumatic family or relationship event, or it can take the form of a communal trauma such as genocide, war or famines, which is passed down through the generations. This communal grief, called 'collective grief', appears to play a major role in generational grief as many people experience these traumas at the same point in time. This grief will have a strong energy field.

Examples of transgenerational grief

An example of transgenerational grief is clearly shown in the study conducted by Yehuda et al., in which they compared the stress-related genes of 32 Jewish people who experienced atrocities under the Nazi regime and those of their children (who were not in the Holocaust) with those of Jewish families that lived outside of Europe during the war.[2] The results showed significant differences between the two groups. The study states: 'This is the first demonstration of an association of preconception parental trauma with epigenetic alterations that is evident in both exposed parent and offspring, providing potential insight into how severe psychophysiological trauma can have intergenerational effects.' (Yehuda et al. use the term intergenerational which is another word for transgenerational.)

This was a groundbreaking study which clearly shows how traumatic events experienced by our parents can affect us on a biological and psychological level.

In the paper '*The American Holocaust: Healing Historical Unresolved Grief*', researchers refer to the appalling treatment of Native Americans by the colonising Europeans. The authors describe how these people were stripped of their land, culture, and way of life, as well as their ability to live in harmony with nature, as they had done for centuries. This negative shift had absolutely dire consequences in the form of deaths, addiction, and family separations. The researchers found that 'Subsequent generations of Native Americans also have a pervasive sense of pain from what happened to their ancestors, and incomplete mourning of those losses.'[3] Two important points were raised. Firstly, that the suffering the children experienced on an emotional level from depression, anxiety, and guilt correlates with those of the findings from Holocaust studies, thus demonstrating the emotional side of generational grief.[4] Secondly, where cultural and ritual grieving and mourning practices were not allowed, several generations of Native Americans have experienced the repercussions of such trauma. This is disenfranchised grief.

In a now famous study conducted by Brian Dias and Kerry Ressler from Emory University in America, mice were exposed to the smell of cherry blossom and then exposed to an electric shock.[5] After repeated instances, the mice would freeze in fear from the cherry blossom smell alone. Whilst this part of the study is a typical example of Pavlovian conditioning, what followed was more significant. The same conditioning of the mice freezing in fear of the cherry blossom alone was retained through at least 5 generations of mice. Great-great grandchildren of the original mice in the experiment responded to the cherry blossom as if they had experienced it themselves. I personally feel that if those who have experienced the original trauma are not allowed to grieve properly or do not work through the trauma experienced, then as a protective/ survival mechanism, the effects of the trauma continue down through the generations much like the mice in the study above until such time as it is resolved. This may be related to what Peter Levine describes in his book *Trauma and Memory* as 'survival-based information', which can be carried down the generations to help them survive should further grief be experienced.

Transgenerational grief, energy, and you

I am sure you are familiar with the medical explanation for how we pass genes down the generations, hence certain medical conditions are described as hereditary. However, from an energetic viewpoint, these gene changes are a result of energetic changes in the body. Energy disruptions in the body change the biology of the body. This is demonstrated in the Yehuda et al. study described at the beginning of the chapter. I call this 'hereditary energy'. Others call it hereditary patterns or epigenetics. Basically, energetic patterns which come down through the generations which hold information about a trauma can have an effect on you here and now; they are literally affecting you today, often without you realising it.

The massive amount of energy produced during loss will certainly affect an individual or a group of people if not dealt with. If your great-great grandfather, for example, suffered a loss that was not dealt with, then this energy is passed down through the generations possibly affecting you. Below is an illustration.

GENERATIONAL TRAUMA / GRIEF

Grief from losing family in a war

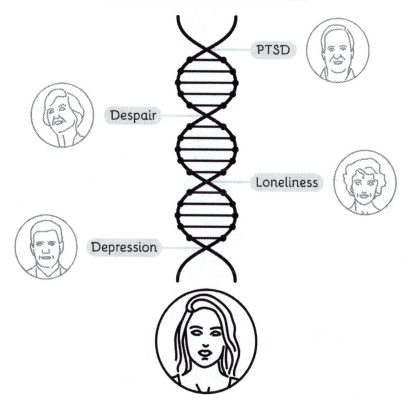

By clearing any shocks experienced around your grief, not only are you helping yourself, but you may also be healing an old generational wound that on some level is affecting you. Additionally, you may be stopping the effects of a long-ago trauma from continuing down your family line. How remarkable is that!

Whatever the reasons as to why transgenerational grief occurs, my main reason for including this chapter is this: if you have, using the content of this book, worked through a lot of your personal grieving experience and have put all that hard work into helping yourself, then it is a good idea to check that generational grief is not part of your journey. For if it is, the potential for it to get in the way of true transformation through your own loss is high. You have done so much work thus far, you do not want to be hindered by long-standing grief from your ancestors.

Life patterns

There are patterns to be seen throughout nature, from the spiral shell of a snail to the markings on a leopard's fur, from the hexagonal shape of the honeycomb to the intricate patterns of a snowflake. Such recurring geometrical shapes and patterns, called fractals, have been studied throughout history. Even our bodies are comprised of geometrical patterns. For example, our blood vessels, lungs, and brain structures are all fractal in nature. Not only are fractals observed in the physical sense, but they are also seen in social organisation, music, and art to name but a few. They also occur in our lives. There will be patterns within your own life, and patterns across the generations. Some would say across past lives, too. Whilst there are both positive and negative patterns, the negative ones will be there as a result of unresolved trauma or grief and can remain until a resolution is found. We will predominately be looking at the more negative patterns, as these are the patterns we are more likely to want to change.

Life patterns are recurring themes – and possibly events – in your life, and while life patterns can take any number of forms, particular patterns, like transgenerational grief, can take the form of emotional issues, physical problems, anniversary incidents, or finding yourself in reoccurring situations that cause considerable upset. Here is an example of each of these:

Emotional patterns could include always finding yourself getting very angry over something very trivial or just regularly getting angry with any number of things. You could find yourself constantly getting into relationships in which anger keeps rearing its ugly head.

Physical patterns could emerge in the form of recurring back, neck, shoulder, or knee problems throughout your life, or you could always be the one to get flu or hay fever every year.

Anniversary incidents could involve having an accident, however large or small, at a certain time of year, every year, or developing a medical issue at the same time each year.

These are a few examples of how patterns can show up in our lives. Many people are simply unaware that there is a pattern to their seemingly random lives. Gregg Braden, among others, has written extensively on the subject of patterns in life; I definitely recommend his book *Fractal Time* if you are interested in this aspect of your grief, as specific timings of particular patterns can be extremely insightful.

> 'To step back and recognize the patterns we've
> lived in the past, and are living right now, is
> perhaps one of the most empowering things we
> can do as individuals and as a civilization.'
> Gregg Braden

Life patterns, emotions, and your loss

While any one of the patterns mentioned earlier may be relevant to you, there may well be patterns around unresolved trauma and grief and you may or may not have been aware of them in terms of patterns. There is a very clear way to gain an understanding of your own trauma/grief patterns and that is by looking at familiar emotions and feelings.

Your own most prevalent emotions and feelings during your grieving journey can be looked at as keys to the doorway of underlying patterns in your life. You filled in your *Healing Heart* with eight common feelings you experienced through your loss. If I were working with you, we would explore whether or not any of those feelings were common or very familiar to you prior to your loss. Say one of those feelings was *disconnection* and you felt this was something you had often felt throughout your life – it was a familiar feeling to you. We would then explore what was going on in your life when you were feeling *disconnected* in the past. Maybe some unresolved past traumas or shocks were shaping your response to grief and now *disconnection* is huge. Not only could previous life events contribute to you feeling disconnected, but you could also be experiencing transgenerational patterns of disconnection. By looking back at which emotions you wrote down on your *Healing Heart*, you might be able to identify a key to your own personal life patterns. Why is this important? Well, to truly transform your life, and help yourself to move from pain to peace, and then beyond to joy, it is a good idea to clear any negative patterns in your life. These patterns come about from undealt-with events due to shocks or trauma (which may or may not be due to your loss); energy is trapped and more often than not a belief is formed. In the example above, it could be 'I always feel so separate from others' or 'I never feel a connection with people'. Then your beliefs become your reality. Clear the shock, shift the belief, and you will be living a life which is far more reflective of your true self than your learnt behaviours.

Here is another example. Laura came to me because of a loss she had experienced. Having lost her mother, we worked through several different aspects of her loss using EFT and Matrix Reimprinting – the shock of losing her mother, the guilt she was feeling about several past events, the sadness about not being able to meet for their weekly coffee, and a specific memory which was really haunting her. She began to really move through these aspects of her loss, but she kept saying she thought something else needed clearing, but she didn't know what. We went back to her *Healing Heart* and found that numbness was a very prominent emotion, so we started doing some tapping around this. Very quickly, several memories came up around when she had had the same numb feeling, and although only a couple were related to loss, the same numb feeling was present in all the memories. We dealt with each of them and Laura's life started to transform. Her numbness had held her back in so many ways and hindered the realisation of some of her dreams. I remember her saying that it felt like a heavy weight had finally been lifted. Laura not only worked her way through her own grief, but was able to transform her life by recognising and changing a paralysing feeling which had held her back. Her loss was the catalyst for transformation. Interestingly, she also recalled her mother had often spoken of a numb feeling too, so maybe she had healed an aspect of generational trauma.

As Joe Dispenza says in his awesome book *Becoming Superhuman: How Common People are Doing the Uncommon*, 'If you're living by the same emotions, day in and day out, your body believes it's in the same environmental conditions. This means those feelings influence you to make the same choices, causing you to demonstrate the same habits that once created the same experiences that produced the same emotions all over again.' Your undeniably painful loss then, shows you, via your emotions, your unique limiting pattern and with it a way to transform your life. Please do not allow the pain of your loss to just slip into a state of suffering and struggle. Use its power and intensity to transform your life and truly honour your lost loved one.

Just a thought…

If, in your *Healing Heart* you scored highly on *anger,* and you feel you were already quite an angry person, it may be that you, as a beautiful soul, have come to Earth to be human and to learn and understand about anger, since you probably wouldn't have much of it running through your pure soul form. Earth is a place to experience human emotions in all their richness. As Bruce Lipton puts it in a video, 'If you're just a spirit, what does chocolate taste like? What does a sunset look like? What does being in love feel like?'[6] While he talks of the positive aspects about life (certainly chocolate is just that), the more painful human experiences can be catalysts for growth and expansion on another level altogether.

What you come into grief with is a reflection of who you were before your loss. Now, however, during your loss, you can change, and your pain can be used to transform your life. You have the potential to shift things. However, if your loss is still raw, perhaps the information that follows is not for you to act upon just yet. I invite you to simply read it now and then come back to it when you feel ready.

Dealing with your life patterns or generational grief with Advanced Clearing Energetics

So what exactly can you do if you recognise that your life pattern or generational grief is negatively impacting your life, or is getting in the way of your grieving process? As you know, you can certainly use EFT and Matrix Reimprinting, and exactly how to do that is shown in the *Self-Love* exercises at the end of this chapter. In addition to these, I want to tell you more about Advanced Clearing Energetics (ACE). (You may remember my personal experience with it at a META-Health workshop – where I was able to leave the toxic relationship I'd got involved in after Andy died? If not, you can check back: it's in chapter 5. It is a particularly helpful technique not for when grief is raw, but when you have moved through your grieving process to a place of peace. As I mentioned, ACE was created by Richard Flook, a true visionary who has spent many years helping people transform their lives. Richard is also the author of *Why Am I Sick: How to Find Out What's Really Wrong Using Advanced Clearing Energetics*. He has conducted extensive research into stress: the role it plays in the body and its impact on psychological and physiological health. ACE is the result of this research. For more information, please look at his website: www.Richardflook.com

ACE is a new and revolutionary way of dealing with all manner of problems and one which I have found extremely helpful for working with patterns within grief. As you will have already gathered by now, energy techniques are fundamental to this book, and therefore fundamental to helping you through your own grief, and ACE is no exception. It is a beautiful and gentle energy technique, which clears and frees painful emotions from life patterns, generational patterns and past lives. It also works in harmony with the other techniques described in this book.

ACE can help you identify patterns in your life by looking at the bigger picture of what you came into grief with. Remember, you do not come into grief as a blank slate. It was not the case that there was nothing going on in your life before your loss. ACE helps to make connections between certain events and how they have made you feel. Understanding these connections, especially negative ones, can help you to identify specific negative patterns in your life, and then gain an understanding about those patterns and clear them. The potential of clearing repeated negative patterns in your life is enormous and totally transformative.

How does ACE work?

ACE works in a totally holistic way, incorporating all of the body. The main premise of this technique, specific to grief and loss, is that the massive stress which losing a loved one can cause is picked up by the heart, the gut, brain, water in the body, and other specific organs. As with META Consciousness, ACE is based on the premise that specific shocks/traumas are related to specific organs, and these organs can react in the form of what we would call a health condition, or disease, ultimately designed to assist the person to solve the stressful event and learn from it. ACE takes you back to before the energy was created, possibly to just before your loss or maybe even to earlier in life, back through family generations or even into past lives. Then the potential to clear the whole of the pattern by locating its true origin can occur. Here is a very brief description: When a sense of being back before the energy of the specific issues is achieved, you then focus into the heart to find out what learnings you could gain from this pattern of energy. Once this is complete and you have some realisations about your loss, then your higher self is called upon to clear that energy. A new energy of something positive is then brought in. I have not provided the instructions here, because they are rather long and detailed; please go to the *Resources* section for more details. I highly recommend ACE. My purpose in this section is to let you know of techniques that can play a significant part in clearing unhelpful energetic patterns.

Joy Beyond Grief – Self-Love Exercise

If you know you are, or feel you may be, affected by generational grief, then firstly I would like to say a huge 'well done!' to you for recognising it. With awareness comes the ability to change. As generational grief can affect you on a physical, emotional, and mental level, to recognise a possible cause is a huge step forward in helping yourself. The next step is about working on the possible effects of that generational grief and how it is affecting your current loss. This will not only help you with what is happening to you at this moment in time, but may well have a positive effect on generations to come as you clear the trapped energy of the past.

Alternatively, you may be unsure if generational grief is affecting your grieving process. The following questions are devised to help bring clarity and give you more insight. However, you may not know the answers about your ancestors – many people don't – and if this is the case, you can work on dealing with what you are experiencing now.

If this whole generational grief thing does not feel relevant to you, then I invite you to go on to the next *Self-Love* exercise on life patterns, which will be relevant to you.

Generational grief

Consider the following questions and make a note in your journal of any of them that resonate with you.

1/ Were any of your ancestors involved in any genocides, wars, or any other major traumatic events?

2/ Are there any group losses in your family history that you know of?

3/ Are you aware of any physical ailments that might have been passed down through generations of your family? Are you also experiencing them?

4/ Are you aware of any emotional/mental problems such as depression, anxiety, or irrational fears, for example, which your parents and their parents before them experienced (or that you yourself are affected by)?

5/ Are you aware of any previous generations who may have experienced unresolved grief?

If you are aware of any of these issues, it is possible that you may be affected by generational grief on top of your own losses in the here and now. It can be one reason why grief feelings can be so, so intense. Or why they are so familiar or why several years after a loss you are still struggling. Remember, you cannot deal with anything that you don't know about or acknowledge, so if anything does ring a bell with you in this chapter, that is a positive move in the right direction. When, or if, it feels right for you, you may wish to do some more detailed family research or you may simply use techniques such as EFT, Matrix Reimprinting or ACE to help shift any stuck energy. This will help you in the here and now with any related physical health and emotional issues or even prolonged grief. It will certainly aid your grieving process to use energy techniques if generational grief is affecting you.

Life patterns

With generational grief, we have looked back beyond your own life; however, life patterns may be more your thing. By looking at your life as a whole, it will help you to understand yourself better and to help make sense of your loss. To explore the concept of life patterns, I invite you to look back at your *Healing Heart*. Take a look at each emotion or feeling to see if it is part of your life patterns. Write each one in your journal and answer the following questions about it.

1/ Are you aware of any patterns in your life either negative or positive?

2/ When thinking about this emotion or feeling, are you aware if it has played a role in any patterns in your life?

3/ Prior to your loss, have there been any other occasions in your life where this emotion or feeling has been prominent? If so, please make a list of those occasions. Can you see any connections?

4/ Does this emotion or feeling seem familiar to you, even if you don't know why?

5/ Is this an emotion or feeling that is often seen in your family?

6/ Do you ever ask yourself, 'Why does this keep happening to me?'

7/ Are there any perceived negative events, situations or experiences which have occurred in your life on more than one occasion?

These questions are designed to help you to gain an insight into any of the negative aspects/events in your life, which may be part of your life pattern. With a greater understanding of your pattern, you are then in a position to make changes. If you do see a pattern or even a bit of a pattern, you can then use one of the energy techniques we've explored to help you to understand and make more sense of your life.

You could now take this information and work with an ACE practitioner (www.richardflook.com), or you could use EFT and Matrix Reimprinting to help yourself with these issues.

If you decide to use EFT, the following will help you proceed.

Chasing the energy exercise

This exercise follows the energy of the emotion/feelings in the body to help you see connecting memories which are part of a pattern.

Step 1 - Decide what pattern or specific emotion/feeling you are going to work on.

Step 2 - If you're still not familiar with the tapping sequence, go back to chapter 6 or watch the video of me tapping on the points.

Step 3 - Now give yourself a rating of intensity about how much that emotion/feeling or pattern is affecting your life as a whole.

Step 4 - Begin with tapping on the SH point whilst saying, 'Even though I have this ………. (Say your recurring emotion/feeling or identified pattern here), I am OK'. Some sample phrases are: 'Even though I have had this repeated issue with anger, I am OK' or 'Even though I can see a destructive pattern in my life which includes feeling low, I am OK'. Repeat your statement(s) 3 times.

Then go around each of the points, saying: 'This …… (your recurring emotion/feeling or identified pattern). For example, 'This repeated issue with despair' or 'This destructive pattern in my life'. Tap approximately 7 times on each point saying this, then move onto the next point until you reach your little finger.

Step 5 - Re-rate your original intensity. Is it the same, has it gone down, has it gone up, has something else come up?

If it's gone down, that's great. Keep tapping to get it right down to zero if you can. If it's gone up, although rare, it can happen, and is usually a sign that a deeper, more hidden, emotion is surfacing, so keep tapping. This is very important. If it's changed, then pursue this new thread of information with the same process as above. It may be that you are spiralling into a more specific aspect of your pattern, which is good, as the more specific you get, the better EFT will work.

Step 6 - See if you can identify where in your body you feel this emotion or pattern. Then, if you can do this, incorporate it into your tapping. For example, 'This despair in my stomach'.

Step 7- Now see if you can add a shape, colour or texture to this emotion or pattern. Then add this into your tapping too. For example, 'This blob of grey despair in my stomach'.

Step 8- Can you recall a memory when you had this 'blob of grey despair in your stomach' before? There may be several memories that come up and they will all be related to this emotion or pattern. Can you see how they are connected?

Step 9- Now you may have found some connections between memories and you can work with your EFT or Matrix Reimprinting practitioners to gain a greater insight into how these patterns have been affecting your life and your grief.

If you get very emotional, remember to use the tap and distract technique. You may then wish to make an appointment with a practitioner, where you can explore and begin to make changes to patterns in your life. This will have a profound effect on you. And remember that there is a gift of grief here: you may not have realised that such emotions/feeling/events in your life were even connected to patterns which can be changed for the better.

Finally, for this chapter's *Self-Love* exercise, we'll be working with your *Transformational Heart*. I invite you to think of ways you may be able to bring these emotions and feelings into your life and begin the process of building a bright new future. This in turn will raise your vibration, opening up further new ways of incorporating such positive feelings, events, or situations into your life, thereby creating new positive patterns.

Here is an example. One of my clients called Brian, who put 'feeling connected' on his *Transformational Heart*, recognised that he could achieve this by getting out more with his friends, and socialising – which he hadn't really done since his grandson had died. The combination of this simple recognition and having worked through the other aspects of his loss helped him feel confident enough to meet up with his friends, which he now does regularly. This connection helped him immensely with his loss. He developed a positive pattern.

So please consider doing the following:

1/ For each of the emotions or feelings listed on your *Transformational Heart*, write a way you could achieve these, preferably regularly.

2/ Discuss them with your grief buddy.

3/ Implement one of them as soon as possible – remember it doesn't have to be a massive event.

4/ Consider introducing a new one at a pace that feels right for you.

5/ Write the events in your journal so you can look back at a later date and see what you've achieved and look at what you could do going forward.

Remember: one small step at a time, go at your own pace and create new healthy patterns in your life.

These *Self-Love* exercises are the beginning of the third part of this book, which is all about the transformation which grief can bring. The negative patterns identified in this chapter as a result of your loss now have the potential to help you make some fundamental shifts in your life. Becoming the best you can be by moving forward into more positive patterns is a beautiful way to honour your lost loved one.

Chapter 11

THE GIFT OF GRIEF

'We acquire the strength we have overcome.'
Ralph Waldo Emerson

Grief can truly be a gift; I invite you to read that again slowly:

Grief … can … truly … be … a … gift.

THIS CHAPTER WAS MORE OF a challenge to write than any of the others. Not because I questioned whether grief could be a gift, but because the forms that those gifts can come in vary so greatly. I am now writing this chapter at another very poignant time in my life. It is now Tuesday afternoon, and last Saturday my mother passed away. She was eighty-six years old. She had dementia, but she always knew who I was, which was a gift in itself. She had some physical issues, and gradually went downhill because of them. The gift, I know already, came to me just three days after her death. And you need to know a little background to our relationship in order to understand this gift.

I never really got on with my mother. We'd never done the mum and daughter things – we never went shopping together, or out for coffee or just for a walk – we did nothing together. I always felt my mum was so self-absorbed, and to me, she never really had time for anyone but herself. If I said we clashed a lot, that would be an understatement. She had been a very fearful person all her life and even she would always joke about how she was frightened of her own shadow.

During her final couple of years of life, she became more and more frail, and with that came a certain vulnerability. Our relationship slowly began to change, and probably for the first time in my life I was able to give her a kiss goodbye whenever I left her at the care home she was living in. Seriously, for years I could not touch her, let alone kiss her, because my anger was so great (totally my issue). Gradually, we began to laugh together and developed a new-found affection for each other. It really was rather funny, and my mother certainly had a good sense of humour (on the rare occasions when she allowed it to shine through). On one occasion when she was poorly in hospital, I gave her a kiss goodbye as I was leaving and she said, 'Bloody hell! I must be dying – you just kissed me!!' We both laughed so much. Our relationship had changed.

In the final few months of her life, we became closer than we had ever been before, and I reached a place of true forgiveness – forgiveness of her, and of myself, of my anger. This is a beautiful, indescribable feeling: a true gift. I believe that having spent time working through my grieving process and following up the other losses I'd experienced cleared the way for me to open up and see the truth of our relationship. I could even see the traits of rebellion and strength that my mother had passed on to me. These traits I am so grateful for: they have propelled me forward in life. In the days before she died, when I was helping her to eat, she even said, 'Janice, you are a good one'. Those words I will never forget.

By the time she passed away, we had got to where we should be. I can honestly say that I now know exactly what forgiveness is *really* all about. I am grateful for actually getting to the place of love with my mother during this lifetime – something which I never thought I would achieve. I began my grieving before she passed, and was able to get to this very special place with her. That is a gift I will always cherish.

That was my gift. Other people's gifts are very different. Remember Deirdre who resolved her painful experiences of being blamed for her young brother's death? After resolving that long-standing stuck energy, her mother was able to tell her how much she loved her and their relationship became a lot closer than it had ever been. Other clients have had gifts in the form of finding out which direction they want their life to go in, be it in terms of where they want to live, or on a more spiritual level, realising that they want to see the world in a new way, or gain a deeper understanding of themselves. Others still have been gifted with a closer connection with those who have passed, by seeing white feathers when thinking of their loved one or even hearing a faint whisper of their name being said in times of need. As you can see, gifts of grief can be very diverse. Later in this chapter we shall explore your potential gifts, but for now I would like you to consider the following questions:

1/ What are your thoughts on the sentence this chapter starts with? ('Grief can truly be a gift.')
2/ Do you think there could be a gift in loss?
3/ Do you wonder how losing a loved one could ever be a gift?
4/ Do you think it was an interesting sentence?
5/ Do you wish it was true?
6/ Do you think *Yes, I believe it can be true,* on some level?
7/ Or do you *know* that it is true?

The way you feel about that sentence is a beautifully clear guide to where you are in your grieving process. Let me explain. If you just don't get it at all, I suggest you are not far enough along in your grieving experience to feel it – and do you know what? That is OK, really it is OK. All I ask is that you consider it as a possibility. Your grieving journey moves along at your pace: grief is not a race. If you follow all the steps in this book, I predict that you will feel differently about this sentence at some point, and when that happens, it will be at the right point for you. Or you may have a quiet belief that this could be possible. Does that mean you are at the right point to hear this message? I feel you might be. Or perhaps you totally understand it, but it has not actually happened yet. Or maybe you are fully aware of your own gift of grief. My dear fellow traveller, all I will say is that if you reach a place of seeing that grief can be a potential catalyst for your own transformation – well, that is a humbling and remarkable place to be.

A check of where you are

Where are you in your grieving experience at this moment? I invite you to answer each of the following questions in your journal:

1/ Have you sought emotional support?

2/ Do you recognise the importance of your emotions?

3/ Have you completed your *Grieving Hearts*?

4/ Have you been using your *Grieving Hearts* to assess any movement in your emotions?

5/ Have you been tapping regularly?

6/ Have you worked through your shock?

7/ Have you dealt with your specific, thorny issues with a trained energy therapist?

8/ Do you understand your life in terms of patterns?

9/ Does your loss ever feel less painful at times?

10/ Do you focus more on the positive memories of your life with your deceased loved one?

11/ Do you have less recall, or at least more neutral recall, of the actual passing of your loved one?

12/ Do you feel ready to reassess where you are and move on to the next stage of your life, knowing that your loved one is never far away?

Did any of those questions reveal a need to do a little more work? Remember, sometimes we need to go backwards *and* forwards a bit. It's all part of our journey.

If you did not answer Yes to all the questions, that is absolutely normal. It just means that you need to look at where you answered No, and give that particular aspect of your grieving process a bit more attention. Go back to the relevant chapter if you need to, or if you feel stuck or unsure, please speak to your trained therapist or contact the *Joy Beyond Grief* network. I suggest that you read on and when you have finished this chapter, go back and do what you need to do.

If you honestly feel that you can say Yes to all those questions, I invite you to ponder and maybe even act upon the information in this chapter. I thoroughly recommend that you do, because having experienced the heart-wrenching pain of loss, and then having used this book to help yourself through your own personal loss, you can make this a pivotal point in your grieving experience. Transformation can really begin to take shape now and the integration of your loss into your life moving forward can occur.

Pain as a catalyst for transformation

Remember when we discussed the vast amount of energy that loss produces? Well, it is that energy that can be a catalyst for transformation – and you can use it to help you to transform, and move your life into a space of love, connection, and any number of positive life changes. For myself, transformation took the form of spiritual growth and although I didn't realise it at the time of my father's death, I was continuously taking steps in that direction. As I explained early on in the book, after he died, I went through times of hating God, to fearing Him, to becoming an atheist, to looking into Buddhism and Hinduism ... I now feel those enquiries were all part of seeking my own spiritual path. On experiencing the loss of Andy, that spiritual path became clearer and clearer to me. Exploring ways to help myself, discovering myself on the way – I call this spiritual growth. I learnt to understand who I was, to feel happier in my own skin, and have a new, fresh view of the world. It is hard to explain, but I suddenly just got it. I used the energy of my loss to help myself transform my life, and I have since found a deep feeling of reconnection and grace. For me, this has been a huge gift.

If I hadn't experienced those losses in my life, could I still have experienced the depth of spiritual growth I found? Obviously, I cannot say for sure. But I am as sure as I can be that I would not have experienced it at the same level of intensity. That intensity made me know that Andy's death was not in vain – that at least some good had come from it. I continue to grow and this is illustrated by the forgiveness I was able to achieve regarding my mother. You may be fully aware of your gift of grief and that is very special – or you may find it will take some time in coming. Be patient, and know it can come in many forms, such as unconditional love, peace, connection, understanding, strength, heightened self-esteem, career change or even a change in location. Whatever your gift entails, it will be right for you. Do not let the pain of your loss be wasted.

Pain equals potential

Allow the pain of your loss to be your teacher, and gain your own personal wisdom. Grief can make us feel as though our life has descended into chaos. Our thoughts become chaotic, our feelings and emotions can also become chaotic, but as Jack Canfield describes, this is simply 'The natural process of chaos that precedes something better.'[1] I clearly do not mean to say that life is going to be better without your loved one, but rather that your life can certainly be transformed as a result of your pain. I invite you to use the enormous amount of energy produced from your loss for a positive transformation in your life: you deserve it.

> 'Of all the maladies that attack the human organism,
> trauma may ultimately be one that is recognised
> as beneficial. I say this because in the healing of
> trauma, a transformation takes place – one that
> can improve the quality of life. While trauma can

be Hell on Earth, trauma resolved is the gift of the
gods – a heroic journey that belongs to each of us.'
Peter Levine

You are stronger than you think

Let's look again at that quote by Ralph Waldo Emerson: 'We acquire the
strength we have overcome.' Journeying through all the chapters in this
book shows enormous strength. The work you have done so far in your
grieving experience – from stepping outside the norm and looking at grief
differently, to following some advice and instructions that may well seem
very odd to you, and then to reach this point in your journey – has itself
taken an enormous amount of strength. The strength shown in achieving
all this has come from the energy of the loss you have experienced. Be kind
to yourself and recognise this huge achievement.

This strength you will now always have. You can't lose it. It isn't going
anywhere. It is something you have acquired, albeit through tragic
circumstances, but then this is where most of us acquire strength from.
Remember the chapter on the difference between pain and suffering? Well,
if you have dealt with your pain, you can use this strength in a positive way
to transform your life, or you can choose to go on suffering indefinitely
and never even realise this strength. Which do you choose? This strength
will help you throughout the rest of your life, if you choose to allow it to.
Here is a wonderful exercise to help you keep engaged with that strength:

Sitting, or preferably standing, either close your eyes or focus them on a
point on the ground in front of you. Move all of your awareness into your
forehead, then pull it towards the back of your head. Imagine that a very
small you is sitting Buddha-style back there. See the space between the
back of your head and your eyes. This is a place of enormous strength,

the gap between you and the world. Whatever is going on in the great pantomime of life is buffered by this space. Being still in this place for a while can help to keep you strong in your mental approach to life.

If there is chaos around you, you can be calm in the back of your head. In Tao, an ancient Chinese way of being, it is said that all our strength is in the back. So, adding on to the exercise above, stand tall, move all your awareness to your spine and become aware of how strong it is, holding you upright in the world. Be kind enough to yourself to see, value, and feel that strength. Be proud of yourself. What you have achieved as you've worked through these chapters is no mean feat. This strength is not in the head – it's not a thinking strength – but a subtler strength of the heart.

Thoughts about your own gifts of grief

As I said at the beginning of this chapter, the gifts of grief can be extremely diverse and individual, and how you access that gift can be just as diverse. I'll elaborate on that. In the last chapter we spoke about life patterns and generational grief. The realisation that these patterns have been occurring can actually be the beginning of your gift, but only if you choose to clear past shocks or patterns which do not support your wellbeing. Clearing the stuck energy from these events will allow you to break free from the shackles of the past and help you step into your future self with all your dreams and desires.

Another realisation is that your loved one will always be there. In previous chapters I have described how clients who have moved through their grieving process come to an inner knowing that their loved ones are not far away. The more you let go of those layers of pain, the more your true self can shine through. The more you see yourself as energy rather than matter, the more the veil becomes transparent between you and your loved one, who is pure energy. The gift can be this realisation.

Maybe your gift of grief is in the form of self-love. Having experienced love with your lost loved one, that deep appreciation for the love you had for them – and still do have – can be a catalyst for you to realise that, perhaps over the years, you haven't been so loving towards yourself. This could be a time to reassess how you can be kinder to yourself. The final chapter will look at this further.

Now spend a moment thinking about your own personal gift of grief. Is it the clearing of old outdated patterns in your life that no longer serve you? Is it the comforting realisation your loved one is never really very far away? Is it a new strength that can lead you towards a change of direction in where you live or your job? Or is it a new-found understanding that being kinder to yourself is a good thing? Or is it something totally different? Whatever it may be, it can be helped along with some heart communication.

It's all in the heart

Now you are at the point in your journey where you have helped your heart to heal by leading it away from the pain, and leading it towards its true nature, guiding you to live a remarkable life. What is amazing is that you have helped yourself, and have helped your heart to heal. Your heart is the core of who you are. With all your practising of heart breathing throughout the book, your communication with your heart has been gently expanded and your general vibration will assuredly be higher.

I remember one of my clients saying to me, 'How do you hear the voice of your heart?' A very good question. Firstly, it can be very difficult to listen to your heart while you are in deep sadness, shock, or any other grief-related emotion. That is why this chapter comes near the end of the book. Also, with society, education, parents, and authority figures all contributing throughout our lives to an endless stream of information that encourages us to use only our brain, our hearts don't often get a look-in until they are shattered with traumas such as loss.

Our conscious awareness has moved away from listening to the heart, preferring to only listen to the head, and boy, oh boy, has the head got a lot to say. Don't get me wrong, our head is superb in actioning anything, but it should be led by our heart's ideas. Our ability to listen to that gentle voice of the heart has, in my opinion, been suppressed to our detriment. Our hearts should be guiding us through life, and our heads should be sorting out the logistics. That's real team work. The wonderful HeartMath Institute, mentioned earlier in the book, are continually working on what they call heart/brain coherence, encouraging the alignment of these two. They state that when the heart and brain are synchronised, the *'body's systems function with a high degree of efficiency and harmony, and natural regenerative processes are facilitated'.*[2]

By listening to our heart, we are far better able to see, feel, hear, and experience those individual gifts of grief. So how do we listen to our heart?

Listening to your heart

Doing the heart breathing exercise you have just done is a perfect way for you to begin tuning into your heart and its infinite wisdom. That said, sometimes in the early days of listening to your heart, there can be confusion between when your heart is talking to you and when fear is talking to you through your mind.

As I mentioned at the beginning, I was brought up by a very fearful mother, and this obviously had an impact on me. I too was afraid of a variety of things for many years. When I started to listen for my heart voice, I was first confronted by my cunning fear voice. For example, I never used to like flying and whenever I was at the airport waiting for my flight, I would hear a voice saying, 'Don't get on that plane. Something is going to happen, it's not safe'. This voice would get louder and more frantic, making me panic even more. Originally, I mistook this for my heart voice. However, as I learnt to identify my heart voice (through practice), I could faintly hear it saying, 'It's all OK, Janice, you are safe, everything is fine'.

Interestingly – and I am only telling you this in case the same thing happens to you – my fear voice then got very clever. It started speaking in a softer tone! It was distinguishable from my heart voice, though I had to concentrate to know the difference. With practice, there is no doubt for me now, and this can be true for you, too. Your heart voice is always loving and supportive, and very gentle, whereas your fear voice can be panicky, harsh, and sometimes not very nice to you.

So, what voice do you hear? Is it one which says, 'Things can never be the same now. Life is never going to be OK again without him/her. I can't believe this has happened to me,' or is there a quieter voice saying, 'Things will be OK. Life will be different, but there is still so much to enjoy'. These may not be the actual words you will hear, but you get the gist. You are aiming to listen out for that gentle, quiet, comforting, and kind voice that can be heard clearly once your fear voice subsides. Remember you can always use your tapping to help with any voice of fear.

Interestingly, as I was writing this, I looked up to see two beautiful buzzards circling above me. I was instantly drawn to thinking of some of the crazy laughs Andy and I used to have. What a wonderful synchronicity. There I was, writing about the heart, listening to the heart and the gifts of grief, when the very first sign I had that I was beginning to live from my heart was that of seeing buzzards. I truly feel gratitude for those precious times Andy and I had together. That love connection with him will always be there and it speaks in the language of the heart. Don't you just love that? When you are living from your heart, beautiful moments like that occur all the time. The knack is to notice them and hear your gentle heart voice.

Joy Beyond Grief – Self-Love Exercise

Heart communication

The heart is light, calm, and can be playful, so I invite you to try the following short exercise. Read it through first, and then try it.

Sit comfortably, relax your body, legs uncrossed, hands resting gently in your lap. Either have your eyes closed for this or fix your gaze on something. Take your awareness to your breathing and gently begin to take a long breath in and a long breath out. Do this a few times. Then do your heart breathing.

Now focus all your awareness into your heart. Imagine taking all of you into your heart and hang out there. What does it feel like? What colour is there? What does your heart want to say to you? You may only get one of these questions answered or you may get something totally different. Just stay playful and see what comes up. Remember your heart responds to a light, fun, loving, warm approach, unlike your head which wants answers now, quickly, and only of the rational variety. Gently open your eyes and come back to the room.

Note down in your journal what you experienced. You may have had many feelings, seen many colours, etc., or you may have only had a few experiences – either way that is perfect. If you didn't feel anything, or your mind started to say things like, 'This is stupid, I can't do this,' or if your mind didn't say anything at all, you will be in the majority, especially if this is new to you. That is your conscious mind trying to talk you out of listening to your heart. It's brilliant in that now you know what that is like, when you do the exercise again, you will be aware of it. Say, 'Thank you, conscious mind, but I am just trying to listen to my heart at the moment, so if you wouldn't mind just sitting over there on that chair right now, we can have a chat later', or something to that effect. Now try the exercise again.

Was that any different? If it was, great, but if not, I would suggest you do some tapping. Possibly the following:

Say, 'Even though my conscious mind keeps trying to butt in when I try to listen to my heart, I am OK' 3 times on the SH point and then go around each of the other points saying, 'My conscious mind is trying to butt in when I am trying to listen to my heart'. Please use the words that are appropriate for yourself. Do that for a few rounds and then try the Heart Communication exercise again. If it changes: brilliant, and if not, try the tapping again. If that seems to have no effect, then I suggest you go back to your practitioner as they will be able to help you with any blocks around this.

You have managed to get a bit of communication going with your heart. Did it feel good in your heart or not? If it felt good, great. If not, again do some tapping – something to the effect of, 'Even though my heart felt dark, I'm OK', 'Even though my heart was dull and heavy, I'm OK'. Either way you had some communication and that is a step in the right direction. If it didn't feel so comfortable there, you may still need to go back to a previous chapter and work on one or more aspects of your loss a bit more, and that's OK too. Perhaps you only got a colour that felt good: well, that's great. Don't try to analyse it. Guess what … that's the brain again. Just enjoy it and know that the more you communicate with your heart, the easier it will become to understand what it is saying.

Transformational Heart - Inner Light Exercise

(You will need your *Transformational Heart* for this exercise.)

Here is a short meditation to help you rebalance your head and heart relationship. Instead of your head always running the show and your heart not getting a look-in, let's work on this by following your heart (your heart's job) and getting your head to sort out the details and implementing your desires (your head's job).

Sit comfortably, relax your body, legs uncrossed, hands resting gently in your lap. Either have your eyes closed for this or fix your gaze on something. Take your awareness to your breathing and gently take a breath in to the count of four and then a longer breath out to the count of six. Do this a few times. Then do your heart breathing.

Once you have settled your awareness on your heart area, visualise a light – a bright warm light that gets bigger and bigger in your heart area. Then allow this light to flow up towards your brain, filling all the areas of your brain before allowing it to flow back down towards your heart and fill your heart. See this light flowing back and forth from your heart to your brain; allow this to happen several times and then, using your *Transformational Heart*, select one of the emotions you wrote; if it's love, bring love into that light and allow it to flow up and down too, or maybe it's peace. Whatever emotion you choose, allow it to flow with the light. When you have done a few rounds, gently bring your awareness back into the room and open your eyes. Have a drink and take your time to get back into your day. Journal your experience.

Chapter 12

THE TURNING POINT IN TRANSFORMATION TO JOY

'Sorrow prepares you for joy. It violently
sweeps everything out of your house, so
that new joy can find space to enter.'
Rumi

AS I WRITE THIS FINAL chapter, I am sitting by a beautiful lake, and looking across it, lush green trees are gently waving to me from the other side of the water. The peacefulness of the lake is a representation of the inner peace I have found. My life has been completely transformed. I love my work helping others, I love spending time with my gorgeous daughters and grandchildren. I love the adventures my partner and I regularly embark upon, and I love my new understanding of life itself and the wonderful planet we live on. I truly believe that you too can experience your own heaven on earth. Hopefully this book has helped you move nearer to this.

In the same video I cited earlier, Bruce Lipton said, 'If anybody has the fondest idea of a heaven, and they're looking elsewhere, I think it's a great mistake. Because your opportunity was to come here to create what you thought you would create in heaven. And because it looks like hell, that's because you bought other people's creations and you have the opportunity to take over your own life and create your own life.'[1]

Your heaven is within you – can you see it? Please don't get me wrong: life throws up its challenges. It always has done and always will do, and don't you know it oh, so well. Loss is incredibly harsh and excruciatingly painful. However, as I have reiterated throughout this book, take things at your own pace and at some point, things can truly transform for the better.

The whole ethos of this book has been about ways to cope, using new tools to help with the emotional pain, and finding peace and understanding. Now we are stepping into the arena of transformation, where we can discover what your grief can bring. It is all about awareness, and what your conscious awareness has learnt from your loss. With this you can pave your way to truly transforming your life.

It is time to think about dreams, desires, and ideas. They may include concepts you have never dreamed of in the past, or not even realised were possible. For me, this moment in my journey was like taking off a set of blinkers. I could see more and then more, and space opened up for more of life's opportunities. I have worked with clients who have found that they felt free to go and travel, to get out and do more things that made their hearts sing, to take up new hobbies, or to simply see the wonders of spending more time with those they love. So where will your journey of transformation take you?

An astonishing event happened to me a few years after I lost Andy. I woke up suddenly, sometime in the middle of the night, and it was pitch black. I quite literally sat bolt upright. I had this immense feeling in my solar plexus area – such a powerful, strong feeling of *Joy* to a depth that I had never experienced before. A *Joy* out of nowhere. It lasted only a few minutes, and even though it was such a remarkable event, once it was over, I simply lay down and went back to sleep.

The next morning, I just had a beautiful, simple acceptance that not only I, but all of us, have the potential to experience more of this, somehow. People have said to me, 'Well, it's obvious what happened. You were just dreaming'. My first response to that is always that it doesn't matter if I was dreaming. It was a profound experience, and so to worry about where it came from is to miss the point. Interestingly, the more time I have had to think about it (it happened around twelve years ago), the more I question how I could have been dreaming about a *feeling* I had never actually experienced before. I understand that we dream all manner of crazy things, but a *feeling* that I had no prior experience of? That's a new one.

I am sharing this experience with you because I wanted to show you just how diverse transformation can be. The feeling I had was from my heart area and as such, I took it to be a heart message. As you've learnt in previous chapters, all heart messages are gentle, calm, and loving, and this experience, whilst extremely powerful, was no different. That is good enough for me. I have not had a similar experience since, and I don't even know what the true meaning of it was. I feel as though Andy might have been involved, but I can't say for sure. However, I do believe that a positive force larger than myself was present. Whatever its origin, it was a wonderful feeling, and I know, I mean *I know* from the heart, that it didn't just come from within me. The feeling seemed to be a message: a message that we can all have more joy – much, much more joy – in our lives, and perhaps experiencing the loss of someone we love can be a catalyst for transformation – and that can be a gift of grief.

This experience happened in the middle of the 'not-so-nice' relationship that I talked about earlier. It didn't change anything at the time, but it did plant a seed which has grown and grown since, enabling me to see life from a different perspective. We transform when we choose to acknowledge our loss and move through and integrate our own grieving experience. Both small and large transformations will be happening all the time. The knack is to notice them, and even better, to celebrate them. Remember, when we celebrate something, we raise our vibration. Have you had any moments of joy? Any moments of feeling the expansion of hope, love, peace? If so, spend a moment recalling them and writing them in your journal. These are your golden nuggets, which will help you to transform your life. Don't underestimate them. And if you can't think of any, don't worry; they will come, or maybe you just didn't notice them. Either way, be on the lookout from now on.

Before proceeding with this chapter, I congratulate you on all that you have achieved as we have travelled through this book together, and I invite you to congratulate yourself too. Firstly, you will have experienced true emotional support, hopefully from a grief buddy who has turned the pages of this book with us. The understanding of your own emotions, and the crucial role that they play in your everyday life, should be clearer to you now. You will have recognised and faced your emotions rather than running away from them, helped along by your *Grieving Hearts*. You will have learnt about tapping, a brilliant self-help tool that you will be able to use any time you need it, and you will have gained an understanding of how the body works from an energy perspective.

You have worked through or at least looked at any shocks that you might have experienced within your loss, and resolved the unresolvable. You have faced those painful persistent memories and feelings. You explored your own beliefs about death, and possibly discovered new ways of looking at it. We have discussed the relevance of generational grief and patterns in your life, and we have discovered what you came into grief with, and how it has been affecting you. You have worked towards clearing any of these patterns that would have been hindering your ability to transform. In the previous chapter, you were introduced to the possibility that grief can be a gift, and learnt how and why you should to listen to your heart.

Let's now move on to how you would like to develop your life from here. How would you like to see your life transform? Have you always had a dream but never fulfilled it? Have you ever had any specific hopes or ambitions that you put aside a long time ago? Has anything become clearer to you while working through this book in terms of which direction you would like your life to be heading? Your dreams are vitally important as they are a reflection of your deepest desires and intentions. These can, however, be buried deeply under years of grief, sadness, and the chaos of any number of other things, but in tuning into them by connecting with your heart, you can envision and create whatever you desire. You truly can.

Unlike other chapters, this chapter will not end with self-love tools. These tools have already been interspersed throughout to help with your transformation, so that you can put them to immediate use to help you along your journey. It is now time to manifest whatever it is that you want to be.

1/ Do what makes your heart sing

> 'New research shows the human heart is much more
> than an efficient pump that sustains life. Our research
> suggests the heart also is an access point to a source
> of wisdom and intelligence that we can call upon to
> live our lives with more balance, greater creativity, and
> enhanced intuitive capacities. All of these are important
> for increasing personal effectiveness, improving health
> and relationships, and achieving greater fulfilment.'
> HeartMath Institute

I once received some fantastic advice, which has grown to become one of my favourite quotes: 'Do what makes your heart sing.' Making your heart sing is how you can guide yourself onto your path of transformation. Once you begin to have communication with your heart, you can begin to *feel* what makes your heart sing. You are looking for a warm, homely, comfortable, zingy-type feeling. Try to tune into how your heart sings. Does singing make your heart sing? Does helping those less fortunate than you make your heart sing? Does writing make your heart sing? I know that there is always something that will make your heart sing – you just need to find it. Begin by being guided by your heart on a day-to-day basis, because when you can truly listen to your heart, you can only succeed. It really is as simple as that. If it feels good, do it and if it doesn't feel good, don't do it. It can take a bit of practice listening for that gentle heart-voice, and often it takes getting past old beliefs such as 'I can't do that because ...' or 'Life just isn't like that'. These sorts of thoughts just come from beliefs which can be cleared with Matrix Reimprinting to allow you to fulfil your dreams and heart-singing desires.

If you are now able to hear that quiet, gentle voice of your heart – the one that only has your higher interests 'at heart' – then you have accessed the beginnings of seeing your loss in terms of being able to transform your life.

2/ Explore your creativity

Creativity is a remarkable tool, both healing and transforming. How do you express your creativity? Being creative is fundamental to our wellbeing, but unfortunately much of our creativity is suppressed from an early age. If, when you were young, your creativity was criticised, you may have created a subconscious belief that you can't be creative, or that your creativity is useless. This belief then becomes who you think you are, and somewhere down the line you realise that you do nothing creative because of a subconscious fear that you will get the same criticism. That is all learnt behaviour and is not who you are; your true self is as creative as every other person on this planet. Everyone has some form of creativity within them. Creativity comes from your soul – it is what makes your heart sing. So, what is your way of being creative?

There are numerous research papers on the health benefits of being creative. For example, in a 2010 study published in the *American Journal of Public Health*, it was shown that along with other positive results, engaging in playing music can calm neural activity in the brain and reduce anxiety.[2]

Let's explore your own creativity. Think for a moment: what did you like to do as a child? Or what have you always fancied having a go at? What do you see others doing that you admire? Any of the answers to these questions can help you find something to be creative with. From drawing and painting to writing and poetry, from creativity in the garden to creativity in the house, from sewing to woodcraft, the creativity list goes on and on. It seems that even the most intense emotions can be utilised in a way that allows for a cathartic release. The pain of your loss can be a catalyst for being creative in whichever way feels right for you – listen to your heart and then follow your heart into your own creativity.

In chapter 2, you were asked to fill in the *Grieving Hearts*, and I have asked you to refer to them several times throughout the book. I invite you to look at your *Transformational Heart* now, and explore the words, feelings, or physical experiences you have written there. These are your wonderful guides on the road to transformation. You may even be experiencing more of them already to some degree, but you can aim to feel more of them, more intensely and more often. It's a creative aim and one you are capable of achieving.

You can make a collage of these words and what they mean to you, if it feels right for you to do so. Start with the one that you marked the highest and work through all of them. Say that you chose the word 'peace' to start with. Write that word down on a piece of paper (as fancily as you want it to be written) and draw a few things around it that represent peace to you. Then, on another part of the paper, write your next word and draw some things it represents to you. Continue with this until you have written all the words from your *Transformational Heart*.

As you are working on each word, really focus on it. You may have supplementary pictures, colours, or other words that come up – anything is fine. No rules! This is your own personal work, and it will act as an inspiration for you as your transformation progresses, allowing you to tune in to these feelings. To get some ideas, here is an example.

COLLAGE OF POSITIVE WORDS

3/ Be kinder

In chapter 1, I explained how kindness can have such a profoundly positive affect on both a giver and receiver – physically, mentally, and emotionally. We have come full circle as I have included it here in this chapter, because kindness can also lead the way to transformation. This means kindness to yourself as well as kindness to others. Make time every day to show yourself some kindness. It may be as simple as reminding yourself how much you care for those around you or reflecting on how kind you are to your animals. If you find yourself speaking negatively about yourself either out loud or in your mind, say '*STOP*' and then say something kind about yourself. The more you do this, the easier it gets. New neural networks in your brain will develop over time and you will begin to change. Self-kindness can take the form of an action like taking a walk, drawing a picture, cooking yourself a special meal -doing something that makes your heart sing is being kind to yourself. The kinder you are to yourself, the more you expand and have clarity about your future enabling you to transform your life. Kindness breeds kindness – being kinder to yourself makes the act of being kind to others flow naturally. If you remember to lead from your heart, you can't go wrong.

Kindness raises your vibration and allows you to truly get in touch with what makes your heart sing. Kindness towards others is another part of your transformation; if you are able to show acts of kindness, you are building stronger relationships and who knows where those relationships may end up? Perhaps new friendships will simply be forged or maybe those relationships will lead you towards a new career or get you involved in some voluntary work you have a passion for.

Whichever angle you want to look at this from, kindness is always the way forward. What act of kindness could you do today for a loved one or even a stranger? Kindness comes in many forms. How creative could you get with those acts of kindness? I also invite you to join in on the act of 'passing a favour forward', so if someone has been kind to you, then you go and do something kind for someone else. This can have far-reaching implications, as acts of kindness ricochet from person to person, communities to communities and from countries to countries. Be kind daily. It's good for your health and wellbeing: physically, mentally and emotionally.

4/ Fill your life with more gratitude

Gratitude is a good friend of transformation. Why? Because when you feel gratitude for anything, you are raising your vibration, and raising your vibration helps you to expand and transform. Many books have been written on how gratitude can positively affect your mind, body, and soul. What do you feel gratitude for? It can be personal or global. It can be small or large. It can be anything you can think of that you feel some gratitude towards. There will always be something if you look hard enough. Having a wonderful friend, hearing birds singing the morning chorus, tasting the warm butter on your toast, feeling your comfortable cosy warm slippers on your feet, or hearing the gentle cascading of a waterfall.

A gratitude exercise

Take a moment and sit still. Feel the ground beneath your feet. Focus on your heart breathing, and imagine bringing a colour into your body and a positive emotion as well. On your in-breath, inhale that colour and emotion and allow them to flow through your body on your exhalation. With your focus on your heart, gently ask yourself the question, 'What am I grateful for?' Allow the natural flow of gratitude to occur. There is no pressure as this may occur slowly or you may be flooded with things to be grateful for. Make a note of them in your journal. It is a good idea to do a gratitude list at the end of each day. This exercise is another one that is simple, yet very effective at keeping your vibration high.

There is an ever-increasing amount of research showing the positive effects of gratitude on physical and mental health. David Hamilton, in the book

I mentioned earlier called *Why Kindness is Good For You*, wrote extensively about the positive effects of gratitude. He cited a study conducted in the US which found that people who regularly wrote down five things they were grateful for were 25 per cent happier than a comparison group who were asked to write down five hassles. This study was only conducted over a ten-week period. Can you imagine what that percentage might have been if it had gone on longer? This is only one of many examples that David cites in his book.

Do you want to try now and see if you are able to feel any gratitude for an aspect of your loss, however small it may be? Do you feel privileged to have been in that heartfelt relationship with your deceased mother, father, sister, brother, child, or friend for however long it was? Are you pleased to have had that last wonderful holiday together? Or that evening you shared together which was full of laughter? Let's try and see if you can add some more things to be grateful for. Sit still and feel the ground beneath your feet, focus on your heart breathing and from the heart, gently ask the question 'What else am I grateful for?' Allow an answer to slowly and gently come forward; do not force it. Savour it, feel it, smell it, touch it, see it, hear it. Then when you are ready, add it to your journal too.

By truly experiencing gratitude, you're taking a huge step towards transforming your life, and here's why. Feeling gratitude helps your body on every level. Gratitude comes from the heart, hence the sayings, 'I thank you from the bottom of my heart', and 'I would like to offer you my truly heartfelt appreciation'. From a physical perspective, it will increase oxytocin (remember our kindness, happy hormone), which in turn will signal to your body that all is well. No fight or flight, no heightened stressful feelings. Your body is calm.

On a mental level, your mind will feel more at ease, clearer, and calmer, as by focusing on gratitude, you will not be experiencing your negative self. Emotionally, you will feel better, since you cannot channel low-frequency feelings at the same time as you are experiencing the higher frequency feelings of gratitude. Your vibration will rise and when this happens, magic takes place, life becomes easier, your dreams begin to take shape and you become more aligned with your truth. The more you hang out in gratitude, the better you will feel. The better you feel, the clearer the way forward will appear.

5/ Forgive more

Forgiveness is the next aspect of transformation that I recommend looking at. I have to say, forgiveness doesn't always get good press, and I think it is because not many people fully understand what forgiveness really means. We all have our own ideas about what forgiveness is – who should be forgiving who, and why we should forgive at all.

Forgiveness can play a major role in grief. Here, I want to take you back with me to the last days with my mother. Initially, I had felt deep peace after forgiving her for the way she had acted towards me. However, it soon became apparent that part of this was about forgiving myself for not having forgiven her sooner. The feeling of peace that came from my forgiving both my mother and myself was a truly profound experience, the impact of which I cannot overstate. This immediately led me to a point where I realised that all was as it was meant to be, and that everything was absolutely fine.

Many clients have come to know forgiveness through their losses in many different ways. For me, it is clear that with true forgiveness comes magic – magic in the form of a deep peace and the honouring of one's self. Conversely, in my experience, those that I have worked with who are adamant that they will never forgive, usually remain bitter and angry, and as we know, this is not helpful when it comes to healing; it can lead to continual suffering.

Does forgiveness play a role in your loss? It may or may not, but spend a few minutes quietly contemplating if there is anyone you would like to forgive, or who you wish to be forgiven by. What I am definitely not doing is asking you to forgive unacceptable behaviour, abuse or such like. I also don't expect you to just forgive people without a true feeling behind it. Forgiveness doesn't work that way. It is a process, but one well worth engaging in for your own benefit. If what you have read has brought up any issues around forgiveness for you, please make a note of it in your journal.

Self-forgiveness is all about self-love. Everyone at some point in their lives says and does things they regret – some minor and some of huge proportions. The point is that it is human to make mistakes, but forgiveness around loss can seem very intense. As I have said throughout this book, be kind to yourself. If you are finding it hard to forgive yourself, consider the following. Did you say or do something to be deliberately hurtful? Maybe you did in a moment of anger and that's understandable. Or did you just lash out because of a build-up of other emotions? That's understandable too. Do you know what? Whatever you say, I am going to reply, 'That is understandable too'. Can you go any small way towards forgiving yourself?

When it comes to forgiveness of others who have hurt you, please remember that it is not necessarily about saying their words or behaviour were acceptable, but instead it is about letting go of the past, so that you can move on to your own transformation. By holding onto past grudges, we make it increasingly difficult to delve deep into our own transformations. Remember that this is still a process. Hey, it took me fifty years to get to this place with my mum, so don't be hard on yourself. This information may just be about planting that first seed of change at this moment in time. Can you plant that first seed, or are you ready to go even further?

Forgiveness, like gratitude, is good for every part of you. It has been shown that those who forgive are at less risk of heart attacks and are less depressed or anxious. I personally believe that forgiveness has a positive effect on both your energy system and your spiritual growth. Reflect on what you have written in your journal. Is holding onto any grudges, be it against others or yourself, helping anyone? Has it affected your health? And what might you do to just make a bit of headway with forgiveness? Go into your heart, for as you know by now, that is the place where all of your questions will be answered. It is all a question of small steps, remember. Small steps. Simply begin with a willingness to forgive. That is a good starting point and you can always use your tapping and work with a practitioner on any issues you feel you need to work on around forgiveness.

6/ Slow down

If you have taken time out to grieve, that is time well spent. It is now time to take time out to allow for transformative ideas to come forward. Time to give yourself space to ask yourself fundamental questions. Here are some that my clients have found useful.

As with so many people, is your life a game of speed, running from one thing to another? Do you really want to be doing all that running around? And not having time for the people you love?

In his book *Inspiration,* Wayne Dyer talked of only engaging in inspiring activities, and how he excused himself from everything else. I am not suggesting that you give up your job and lifestyle; I'm just suggesting that you take a good look at what you actually enjoy and what you don't. Let some things go if you can. Freeing space in your diary means freeing space in your mind. This means a calmer and happier heart, mind, body, and soul. Slowing down is all about being mindful of your thoughts, feelings, and behaviours. As you learn to be more mindful of who you actually are, you will increase your self-love and develop a deep wisdom from within, which can guide you to beautiful transformations you hadn't even considered.

Certainly, one way to slow down is to do what you have just done – your heart breathing exercise. It can simply give you that moment of presence, a moment where you are really in the here and now. That is a good way to start slowing down. With all your attention right here, right now, and no reflecting on the past or projecting into the future, you allow your mind and body to relax a little. Creativity, kindness, and gratitude, as previously discussed, are all superb ways to help yourself slow down too. Often when we lose people, we want to keep doing, doing, doing but that, as was also discussed, is not conducive to helping you with your loss.

Previously I encouraged you to stop and take stock of your emotions and feelings and then I provided you with tools to help. But here, at this part of your journey, I invite you to start focusing on being, being, being – not doing, doing, doing. After all, you are a human being, not a human doing. I invite you to think of ways you could slow down, take time for yourself, and make some changes. Maybe write two lists: one of things in your everyday life you love and that make your heart sing, and the other of things you feel you have to do. Gently, and from a heart-centred space, start playing around on paper or in your head with areas of your life you would like to see a difference in. What would you like to do more of? What would you like to do less of? This will give you a good guide to *being* more and *doing* less. Maybe use a mantra. One I love is 'Move towards what makes your heart sing and away from what doesn't'. One small step at a time and before long you will see your life transform before you.

7/ Meditate

Meditation can be an expanding and transformative practice. People from every part of the world have practised meditation for many thousands of years and it has been shown time and time again to benefit the mind, body, and spirit. Although it is not advisable to practise meditation immediately after loss, once the shock has been dealt with, it becomes an increasingly helpful tool – especially when talking of transformation.

The many benefits of meditation are far too numerous to name in full, but here are a select few: pain relief, better sleep, strengthened immunity, better digestion, lower blood pressure, better circulation, lower stress levels, improved ability to cope with stress, better focus, reduced mind chatter, improved memory, better mind-body connection, reduced anxiety and depression, emotional stability, productivity, inner silence, promotion of spiritual awakening, increased compassion, and the feeling of being more present. So it may be worth giving it a go?

Meditation is like a long, warm bath for the soul. If you have never meditated before, I recommend that you follow a short, guided meditation to start with, as this really helps you to keep focused (you can follow my meditations on my website www.janicethompson.co.uk). Gradually, and at your own pace, you can increase the length of each meditation. Play around with what suits you: every day, every other day, for two minutes, fifteen minutes or for a full hour if that suits you, but just start gradually and build up. You can even join a meditation group, which is also an excellent way to meet new, like-minded people. Online, there are many wonderful sites where meditations are free, so try them out. Listen to your heart for the one that feels right for you in that moment. I cannot recommend meditation highly enough, and in terms of your transformation, it will allow you space, clarity, and help you slow down for long enough to start to consider what you want from your life from this point onwards.

'The thing about meditation is: You
become more and more you.'
David Lynch

8/ Love yourself ... more

Here we go with the biggie. Self-love is what it's all about. Louise Hay (an icon in the self-help world) said, 'You can't do anything well or for the long term without loving yourself first.'[3] There you have it straight from the horse's mouth. The more self-love you have, the easier, more contented, and more enlightened and exciting your life will become. Everything in this chapter is about self-love.

Self-love is a major aspect of transformation. Giving yourself time to be creative is about self-love, acknowledging things you have gratitude for is self-love, forgiveness is a self-loving act, as is kindness. Slowing down and meditating are actions of self-love too.

Unfortunately, historically self-love has been used in connection – or even worse used interchangeably – with the word *selfish*. All the negative connotations that go along with that word often meant that self-love has had a bad press too. This negativity has become a part of our society. We learnt at a young age from parents, schools, authority figures, and community groups, not to be selfish or to love ourselves. However, I am pleased to say this is definitely changing, and the subject of self-love is now being discussed in more positive terms.

It is obviously not just about caring for yourself and to hell with everyone else (as the word selfish may imply). It is about addressing how skewed our thoughts and feelings have become about ourselves. Self-loathing, hating yourself or simply and constantly putting yourself down whilst trying to live up to unrealistic expectations have now become commonplace. However, the world is waking up, and many people throughout the world are realising the benefits and importance of self-love. Simply being kinder to yourself and making time for yourself has the knock-on effect of many health benefits too. Along with healthy individuals who understand the true meaning of self-love come healthier, kinder, happier communities and subsequently a more peaceful, loving world.

So now, having established that self-love is a positive thing, how kind are you being to yourself? How much time do you give to your own self-love? How high on your list of priorities do you rate self-love? Do you feel you deserve to be loving towards yourself? Do you ever find yourself forgiving others when you wouldn't forgive yourself for the same thing? By simply making a note of these questions in your journal, you will become consciously aware of where you are in terms of self-love.

Self-love comes in many forms and is very individual; however, it is wise to incorporate the mind, body, and spirit. Let's begin with self-love for the mind. Again, whenever you catch yourself saying anything negative to yourself, I want you to say 'STOP' in your mind, and immediately think of something that is the opposite and loving towards yourself. For example, if you hear yourself saying 'I'm useless. I just can't get myself together after the loss of ...' then I want you to say 'STOP' and say to yourself something like 'I am OK and I am doing the best I can'. It doesn't have to be directly related to the negative thought – it can be something general and that is equally fine. This is all about retraining your brain to refocus on the positive – not negative – self-talk, and as we've seen, with practice, your brain will begin to rewire itself with these positive comments and they will begin to override the negative self-talk as new neural pathways develop.

Self-love for your body

I am not a gambling lady, but if I were, I would probably lay a bet on it being easier for you to tell me what you don't like about your body as opposed to what you do like about your body. Does that sound right? I feel we are all heavily influenced by the media and peer pressure when it comes to how we think we should look. Often, these ideas are totally unrealistic, and in my opinion undesirable. Spend a moment looking in the mirror and try to find at least one thing you do love, and I mean *love* about your physical self. Can you do that? If you can, great! But if you can't, can you find one thing you are OK with about yourself? However small, that is fine.

Every time you are unkind to your body, say 'STOP' and take your focus onto the one thing you do love (or like) about your body. This will also help you to rewire those pathways that have got so used to you being so unkind towards yourself. If you are able to say a few things, that is great: just mix and match them if anything negative comes up. However, if you can't say anything kind towards yourself, know that you are not alone. Don't beat yourself up: it can be hard to love your body. Accept where you are as your starting point and gently shift things. But if you truly want to transform your life, this is where things can begin to change. Go into your heart and do your heart breathing and see if any small things come up. It can be as small as 'I quite like my fingernails', or 'My eyebrows aren't so bad'... anything is great. Please keep looking: you will find something.

Self-love of the body also includes eating natural and healthy foods, and doing some exercise. With regards to eating, there is a lot of wonderful information out there about all you need to know about food, with people far more qualified than I am to guide you, so go and explore new cuisine (that's a self-love exercise in itself).

An area I am familiar with is exercise, as I used to be a personal trainer. There are the obvious physiological benefits of exercise including an improved cardiovascular system, increased muscle tone, increased flexibility, reduced resting heart rate, reduced blood pressure, improved glucose metabolism, improved cholesterol ratios, increased lung capacity, and I could go on.

There are also many psychological benefits. These include improved mood, a better ability to cope with stress, an improvement in self-esteem, an improved body image, an increase in energy, and an increased satisfaction with oneself. I definitely recommend some form of exercise to help you with your transformation. Specifically, I promote being out in nature. Getting your body out in nature as discussed in the first chapter will not only be beneficial for your body on a physiological level, but it is so good at lifting your mood. Even if you can't get out and about, you can do some simple seated exercises at home; you can find some awe-inspiring scenes (on the internet or in a book) – enlarge them and spend time immersing yourself in them. Or why not try listening to sounds of nature as these have been shown to decrease stress hormones and improve immune function. Being in natural surroundings helps raise your vibration and in turn this can inspire your mind and spirit to tune into new ways of living your life.

Self-love for your spirit

Just how do you do that? Meditation is definitely a major part of this aspect of your self-love: being still and quiet allows for the messages from your higher self or soul to come through your heart and into this life and they will always be guiding you towards self-love. Allowing your soul to step forward via your heart gives you the means to truly begin to create your own destiny. If you follow your inner wisdom, self-love will blossom and the most extraordinary dreams can come true. Use the strength you have gained to help yourself push through your comfort zone and beyond to a true transformation of you and to a place where joy resides inside you.

9/ Manifest what you want

In a wonderful book by Richard Dotts called *It Is Done*, Richard discusses manifesting in great detail and how to manifest what you want. It is a book worth reading. One of the main points he puts across is how our worry, fear, impatience, and distrust can get in the way. As you and I have worked together, I have encouraged you to look at your emotions and I am sure that you have already dealt with some of your worries and fears.

Doing this will help you in your endeavour to manifest your life the way you want it. With regards to impatience, I feel that working through your loss has certainly shown you are able to be patient. The block of distrust can certainly be a challenging one when you have lost a loved one and the universe seems like a very untrustworthy friend; however, having worked through and had time to consider your loss in a spiritual way, hopefully you have gained back some trust in the universe.

If, according to Richard, you are able to deal with these four blocks, then your ability to manifest is greatly increased. Your experience of loss has enabled you to look at the issues which make up each of these blocks. So, the world better look out: you are about to start manifesting your life as you want it! There are many different exercises which can help with manifesting. They include visualisation boards, where you put all your ideas on a board and keep adding to it and checking it regularly. You could also use affirmations, posted around your home, of dreams you wish to achieve.

Here is one final *Self-Love* exercise:

1/ Give yourself time and space where you will not be disturbed.

2/ Sit quietly and ground yourself. You can use the tree root visualisation (imagining your feet to be firmly planted in the ground and roots coming out from them spreading wide and deep into the Earth), or you can imagine yourself connecting to your higher self (imagine a light going up through your crown chakra connecting to your higher self) or do both. Neither of these are essential, but they will help you to stop whatever you have been doing and focus on manifesting.

3/ Do a few heart breaths so that your mind, body, and spirit are all in harmony.

4/ State what it is that you want to manifest. Do start with something small. Manifesting is an art. It takes practice before it can be perfected, so don't try and run before you can walk, so to speak. Be specific and clear.

5/ Finish with a finalising word or statement. Some people say *Amen, it is done*, or *So it is*. Say what feels right for you, but know the importance of this step. You are handing your command over to the universe, so you must really say it with conviction.

6/ Let it go. Once you have said your finalising word or statement, let it go. Give no more attention to when or where it will happen. It can be helpful at this point to take your focus to a nice place in your mind (maybe a lovely garden scene or a beach, etc.), and just hang out for a few moments, using all your senses to be in this place.

Remember, manifesting is an art, and something which is very individual, but if you have removed your blocks, have a clear intention, have said your finalising statement and really let it go, it is simple. If it doesn't work, it simply means you haven't quite mastered it yet and that's OK too. This is a work in progress. Or maybe another form of manifesting would suit you better: look around at the many books on this subject. Finally, keep it light and playful, not heavy and demanding.

I have suggested nine ways to help you to transform your life. There are many more, but those I have given provide a good foundation to help you. (They can be used with children in an age-appropriate way.) This is the point where you can really congratulate yourself: you are a remarkable person and have gone through a grief that only you truly know. Hopefully this book has given you some knowledge, tools and strategies to help you through your own grieving experience, enabling you to find peace, and beyond that, to see that the pain of loss can be a catalyst for transformation. Whilst these may be the final few words of the final chapter in the book, it is only chapter 1 of the rest of your life. Your loved one will never be forgotten and will always be with you moving forward. Honour this journey, knowing your loved one has always been, and is, close by, just on the other side of a thin veil.

The time you and I have spent together may have been a relatively short one, or it might have lasted a few years in terms of actually following all the steps we have gone through. Either way I wish you love and peace for all that you are and shall become.

Death is not all that it seems

Janice Thompson

Death, death is not all that it seems,
Not a bitter blunt ending of our hopes and our dreams,
Not a nightmare butting in on our tranquil slumber,
Not a freak in the night,
A lightning strike, crash of thunder.

Death, death is not final nor a giant full stop,
But a comma, a pause, in the soul journey's book,
Not the final chapter in the tragedy of life,
But a speck on the page,
Barely seen by the eye.

Death, death is not cold or alone,
But a spark of divine, from our house to our home,
From dark drapes and dull walls
To a palace of bliss,
A playground of love where we dance and we kiss.

Death, death is never goodbye,
Just a soul moving on from this illusion, this lie,
So let's wish those souls well and not mourn and not cry,
But rejoice and send love,
On their journey through time.

TESTIMONIALS

Janice is one of the most authentic, kind and inspirational people I have met in this field of work. She truly embodies her work, and her compassionate way of teaching, training and working with clients is something I have witnessed both professionally and personally. She is an expert in the field of grief and her knowledge is something to be valued in an area where this open way of thinking is so needed. I am blessed to call her a colleague and a friend.

Catherine Banks MSc.
Meditation & Reiki trainer & EFT therapist / Grief specialist
https://www.catherinebanks.co.uk

Janice is the most loving, kind, compassionate soul that you could wish to meet, and through her journey of sudden unexpected loss and grief she has navigated her way, exploring many different techniques coupled with personal and professional experience with a whole load of research too. She is a true expert in the field of grief; her knowledge and expertise are second to none. She has incorporated all of her specialist grief courses in this book, making it a wonderful supportive, transformational tool to help you to find the Joy Beyond Grief. *Having been on a similar personal path with loss and grief, I can't recommend Janice and her book highly enough. I have known Janice for many years, and she lights up any room with her energy with so much fun and joy of life. She has made talking about grief become so accessible which is so important as it is not a conversation or topic that many feel comfortable with. I specialise in working with mothers on all aspects of their motherhood journey and Janice's work and support have been invaluable.*

Lisa Barry
https://www.amothersawakeningjourney.com

This is one for your 'active bookshelf'. Janice has been the authority on grief and loss, helping hundreds of clients navigate their way through their unique healing journeys, and also delivering specialist EFT practitioner trainings of sheer excellence. I know – I've been the recipient of both and am so grateful for the enormous difference Janice has made to my own life, and also to my own practice and those of us on the FAST team. Now, with her book, Janice has also become an author authority, allowing her skills and brilliance to reach a wider worldwide platform.

Wendy Power Stoten
Stoten Founding Director of FAST Trauma Support CIC.
https://www.fasttraumasupport.org.uk/

Janice is one of those genuine souls who shines a light not just of hope, but the real possibility of joy to anyone negotiating the journey of grief.

Her incredible compassion, unique perspective on the journey through grief and practical self-help tools based on her own experience and work with clients is beautifully encapsulated in this book, which is one of those rare gems: a ray of hope to all who read its pages.

With heartfelt thanks, Janice, for all you to do inspire those on a journey through grief towards joy.

Andrea Bird BSc (Hons)
Soul Guide & Energy Psychologist
https://bamazingu.com/

Janice Thompson has a unique approach to grief and loss, and she brings her extensive experience, passion and drive to this much-needed and timely book. Her insight has helped me enormously, both on a personal and professional level.

Wendy Lydford
thecoreofthematter.co.uk

Janice can only truly be described as a walking angel. I have been privileged to benefit from her knowledge, empathy, openness, kindness and compassion as I dealt with the unexpected loss of my darling grandmother in 2018. I was incredibly lucky to have been able to road test many of the exercises detailed within the chapters of this book and I can honestly say, I don't know how I would have been able to effectively manage my grief alongside a full-time role building my company and the completion of my MBA studies without it. That said, over the years I have worked with Janice, the loss of my grandmother is not the only thing I have dealt with. Loss of contracts, investments, friends, and love interests have all come up and the tools offered here have helped me immeasurably in bouncing back from them all. There are few books that can genuinely create monumental change in your life... This is most certainly one of the few.

Erika Brodnock
Founder of Kami
www.usekami.com

JOURNALING SPACE

JOURNALING SPACE

REFERENCES

Chapter 1: Emotional Support

[1] Hamilton, David. 2010. *Why Kindness is Good for You*. Hay House.

[2] Pennebaker, James, Zech, Emmanuelle and Rimé, Bernard. 1988. 'Disclosing and sharing emotion: Psychological, social and health consequences.' *Child Development*, Dec;59(6):1580-9.

[3] Parkes, C.M. 1964. 'Recent Bereavement as a Cause of Mental Illness.' *The British Journal of Psychiatry* Mar 110 (465) 198-204.

[4] https://www.berkeley.edu/news/media/releases/2009/12/08_survival_of_kindest.shtml

[5] Mind Week Report. 2007. 'Ecotherapy: The green agenda for mental health.' *Mind*.

[6] Mitchell, R. and Popham F. 2008. 'Effect of exposure to natural environment on health inequalities: An observational population study.' *Lancet,* 372 (9650), 1655-1660.

Chapter 2: Feelings and Emotions: Ignore or Embrace?

[1] McLaren, Karla. 2010. *The Language of Emotions*. Sounds True Inc.

[2] Lipton, Bruce. 2005. *The Biology of Belief*. Hay House.

[3] Lipton, Bruce. 2005. *The Biology of Belief*. Hay House.

Chapter 3: The Shock of Loss

[1] https://www.brucelipton.com/blog/what-do-you-know-about-your-conscious-mind-the-creator-within

[2] Mojica, Gamal Salim Paez. *2019.* 'Disruptions of the energy field and illness.' *Journal of Nursing and Care*. March 25-26, 2019.

Chapter 5: Everything is Energy

1   Polich, Judith Bluestone. 2001. *Return of the Children of Light*: *Incan and Mayan Prophecies for a New World*. Bear & Company.

2   McTaggart, Lynne. 2003. *The Field: The Quest for the Secret Force of the Universe*. Harper Collins Publishing.

3   Dawson, Karl, and Marillat, Kate. 2014. *Transform Your Beliefs, Transform Your Life*. Hay House UK Ltd.

4   Wilcock, David. 2012. *The Hidden Science of Lost Civilisations*. Souvenir Press.

5   Sheldrake, Rupert. 2009. *Morphic Resonance: The Nature of Formative Causation*. Icon Books Ltd.

6   The Global Coherence Initiative. https://www.heartmath.org/articles-of-the-heart/global-interconnectedness/global-coherence-initiative/

7   McCraty, Rollin. 2015. *Science of the Heart*. HeartMath Institute.

Chapter 6: Time Will not Heal, but Tapping Will

1   Stapleton, Peta. *The Science behind Tapping*. 2019. Hay House.

2   Geronilla, L. et al. 'EFT (Emotional Freedom Techniques) remediates PTSD and psychological symptoms in veterans: A randomized controlled replication trial.' *Energy Psychology: Theory, Research, and Treatment* 8, no. 2 (2016): 29–41.

3   Church, D., Stern, S., Boath, E., Stewart, A., Feinstein, D. & Clond, M. 2017. 'Emotional Freedom Techniques to Treat Posttraumatic Stress Disorder in Veterans: Review of the Evidence, Survey of Practitioners, and Proposed Clinical Guidelines.' *Permanente Journal*. 21:16-100. Published online 2017 Jun 22. doi: 10.7812/TPP/16-100

4   Church, D., Yount, G., & Brooks, A. J. 2012. 'The effect of Emotional Freedom Techniques (EFT) on stress biochemistry: A randomized controlled trial.' *Journal of Nervous and Mental Disease,* 200(10), 891-896.

5   Church, Dawson, De Asis, Midanelle, and Brooks, Audrey. 2012. 'Brief group intervention using EFT (Emotional Freedom Techniques) for depression in college students: A randomized controlled trial.' *Depression Research & Treatment* doi:10.1155/2012/257172

6   Chatwin, H., Stapleton, P.B., Porter, B., Devine, S., & Sheldon, T. 2016. 'The Effectiveness of Cognitive-Behavioural Therapy and Emotional Freedom Techniques in Reducing Depression and Anxiety among Adults: A pilot study.' *Integrative Medicine,* 15(2), 27-34.

7   Gill, J.M., Saligan, L., Woods, S. & Page, G. 2009. 'PTSD is Associated with an Excess of Inflammatory Immune Activities.' *Perspectives in Psychiatric Care.* https://doi.org/10.1111/j.1744-6163.2009.00229.x

8   Bach, D., Groesbeck, G., Stapleton, P., Sims, R., Blickheuser, K. & Church, D. 2019. 'Clinical EFT (Emotional Freedom Techniques) Improves Multiple

Physiological Markers of Health.' *Journal of Evidence-Based Integrative Medicine.* 24. doi: [10.1177/2515690X18823691](10.1177/2515690X18823691)

9   Stone, B. et al. 2010. 'Energy Psychology Treatment for Orphan Heads of Households in Rwanda: An Observational Study.' *Energy Psychology, Theory, Research & Treatment.* 2 (2). Pg.31-38.

Chapter 7: Resolving the Unresolvable

1   Lee, J.L.C. et al. 2017. 'An update on memory reconsolidation updating.' *Trends in Cognitive Science.* July; 21(7); 531-545.

2   Nader. K. et al. 2000. 'Fear memories require protein synthesis in the amygdala for reconsolidation after retrieval.' *Nature.* Aug 17; (6767): 722-6.

3   Stewart, A. et al. 2013. 'Can Matrix Reimprinting Be Effective in the Treatment of Emotional Conditions in a Public Health Setting? Results of a Pilot Study.' *Energy Psychology Journal.* 5 (1).

Chapter 8: Beliefs, Spirituality, and the Soul

1   http://www.getmotivation.com/drwdyer.htm

2   Pearsall, Paul. *Super Joy.* 2012. White Crow Books.

3   Schutzenberger, Anne Ancelin. 2009. *The Ancestor Syndrome.* Routledge.

4   Northrup, Christiane. 2018. *Making Life Easy: A simple guide to a divinely inspired life.* Hay House.

Chapter 9: Grief and Physical Wellbeing

1   https://www.bbc.co.uk/news/magazine-36213249

2   Bradbeer, M. et al. 2003. 'Widowhood and other demographic associations of pain in independent older people.' *Clinical Journal of Pain.* Jul-Aug; 19 (4): 247-54

Chapter 10: Transgenerational Grief and Life Patterns

1   Schutzenberger, Anne Ancelin. 2010. *The Ancestor Syndrome.* Routledge.

2   Yehuda, R. et al. 2016. 'Holocaust Exposure Induced Intergenerational Effects on FKBP5 Methylation.' *Biological Psychiatry.* Sept 1. Volume 80, issue 5, 372-380.

3   Yellow Horse Brave Heart, M., and DeBruyn, L.M. 1995. 'The American Holocaust: Healing historical unresolved grief.' *American Indian and Alaska Native Mental Health Research* Copyright: Centers for American Indian and Alaska Native Health. Colorado School of Public Health/University of Colorado Anschutz Medical Campus (www.ucdenver.edu/caianh)

4   Levine, Peter. A. 2015. *Trauma and Memory*. North Atlantic Books.

5   https:// newscientist.com/article/dn24677-fear-of-a-smell-can-be-passed-down-several-generations/

6   https://www.youtube.com/watch?v=LoJx_q2r7SI

Chapter 11: The Gift of Grief

1   Canfield, J. cited in Massey, Harry & Hamilton, David. 2012. *Choice Point: Align Your Purpose*. Hay House.

2   McCraty, Rollin. 2015. *Science of the Heart*. HeartMath Institute.

Chapter 12: The Turning Point in Transformation to Joy

1   https://www.youtube.com/watch?v=LoJx_q2r7SI

2   Stuckey, H. L., and Nobel, J. 2010. 'The Connection between Art, Healing and Public Health: A review of current literature.' *American Journal of Public Health*. February; 100(2): 254-263 https://www.ncbi.nlm.nih.gov/pmc/articles/PMC2804629/

3   Hay, Louise. 1984. *You Can Heal Your Life*. Hay House.

RESOURCES

For supporting material for this book including video meditations, crystal layout packages, and an additional *Healing Hearts* supporting workbook, please go to www.janicethompson.co.uk

Chapter 1

The HeartMath Institute research the heart's intelligence by connecting heart and science to help people to reduce their stress levels. Their research has shown just how much of a positive impact heart breathing has on your body. They also have some practical tools that expand on this heart breathing method, should you wish to take this further. Please visit their website for more information: www.heartmath.com

Chapter 2

To download the *Grieving Hearts* workbook, please go to my website: www.janicethompson.co.uk

Chapter 3

There are numerous studies which show how stress can affect the body physically. Some examples are below:
https://www.healthline.com/health/stress/effects-on-body#2

Wirtz, P. H., and Känel, R. 2017. 'Psychological Stress, Inflammation, and Coronary Heart Disease.' *Current Cardiology Reports.* 19, 111.

Fagundes, C.P., and Wu, E.L. 2020. 'Matters of the Heart: Grief, Morbidity, and Mortality.' *Current Directions in Psychological Science.* https://doi.org/10.1177/0963721420917698

Thimm, J. C., Kristoffersen, A.E., and Ringberg, U. 2020. 'The prevalence of severe grief reactions after bereavement and their associations with mental health, physical health, and health service utilization: a population-based study.' *European Journal of Psychotraumatology.* https://doi.org/10.10 80/20008198.2020.1844440

Robert Scaer is a neurologist who has contributed greatly to the study of traumatic stress and its role in emotional and physical syndromes and diseases. He has written several books including *The Trauma Spectrum: Hidden Wounds and Human Resiliency*, *The Body Bears the Burden: Trauma, Dissociation and Disease*, and *8 Keys to Brain-Body Balance*.

Chapter 5

The HeartMath Institute research the heart's intelligence by connecting heart and science to help people to reduce their stress levels. Their research has shown the connections between people and animals. Please visit their website for more information: www.heartmath.com

Crystal therapists work with crystals and can help you with your grieving process. Reputable therapists can be found at https://www.crystalcouncil.org/. An extremely well-qualified crystal therapist I would recommend is Lauren D'Silva; she can be contacted at https://www.crystal-therapy.co.uk/

Colour therapy is a therapy which can help with your grieving process. Colour mirror therapists work with bottles of coloured oils and essences; a reputable therapist can be found at https://www.colourmirrors.com/ I would personally recommend Lisa Barry and she can be found at https://amothersawakeningjourney.com/

Chapter 6

EFTi https://eftinternational.org/ A resource for research articles and many aspects of EFT.

EFT and Mindfulness Centre https://www.eftandmindfulness.com/ articles/eft-research. A resource for EFT information and research articles.

Below is a poem I wrote for children to use to get used to tapping: you can do it with them. Then, if they become upset, they already know the technique to use to help themselves.

The Magic Tapping Adventure for Children

Start the tapping on the side of your hand,
The top of your head, your next tap should land,
To the eyebrow we must go
And the side of the eye, not the toe!!
Under your eye is feeling left out
Then under your nose or if you're an animal, your snout,
Tap tap tap under your lip
From your head to your body, now you will skip.

Tap tap tap if you're angry or sad
Tap tap tap if you're unhappy or mad!!
Tap tap tap if you're feeling unwell
Tap tap tap if you don't want to come out of your shell
Tap tap tap if you're happy too,
Tap tap tap just for you.

We must tap on a place that's hard to find:
Just ask someone to help, they won't mind!
It's found each side of the knot on a tie,
Tap with both hands, then on we shall fly
To under the armpits, like a monkey we'll be
Now down to the hands: come on! Tap them with me!

Tap tap tap if you're angry or sad
Tap tap tap if you're unhappy or mad!!
Tap tap tap if you're feeling unwell
Tap tap tap if you don't want to come out of your shell
Tap tap tap if you're happy too,
Tap tap tap for you.

Let's start on the thumb, tap, tap by your nail
Not too fast, but not as slow as a snail!
Then onto the fingers: tap on each one,
Being kind to each finger until they are all done.
The magic tapping adventure is now complete
Or you can do it again, but not on your feet!!!!

Tap tap tap if you're angry or sad
Tap tap tap if you're unhappy or mad!!
Tap tap tap if you're feeling unwell
Tap tap tap if you don't want to come out of your shell
Tap tap tap if you're happy too,
Tap tap tap for you.

Further resources for children

I have a wonderful friend and colleague, Erika Brodnock, who has developed an excellent, award-winning brand called Karisma Kidz, which helps children to understand their emotions. This is definitely worth looking into if you have children. It will not only help with their grief, but will also help them to develop healthy emotional wellbeing: http://karismakidz.co.uk/

Books for Children

Gorilla Thumps and Bear Hugs by Alex Ortner

The Wizard's Wish by Brad Yates

Hug Your Heart books by Bryony Irving

Another close friend and colleague, Wendy Lydford, has made several excellent short YouTube videos for tapping with children. They can be found at http://www.thecoreofthematter.co.uk

Chapter 7

For Matrix Reimprinting Practitioners please go to: https://www.matrixreimprinting.com/practitioner-directory.aspx

The American grief educator, Dr Louis LaGrand, specialises in this area, and he has written several books that promote what he has called 'barrier-transcending' exercises similar to the one described in the *Self-Love* exercises in Chapter 7. Please look him up at: http://www.extraordinarygriefexperiences.com/

Chapter 9

For more information about META-Health in general and including eczema, please go to: https://www.meta-health.info/meta-health/ . However, I would personally recommend a former Master trainer with META-Health: Penny Croal. Penny is an extremely knowledgeable therapist and trainer who has developed her own understanding of bio-psycho-social connections, known as META Consciousness. For more information, please go to: https://www.changeahead.biz/work-with-me/meta-consciousness-analysis/

Chapter 10

ACE, developed by Richard Flook, is an excellent technique used for life patterns you would like to change. The technique itself can be quite long. So, to get an idea as to whether it is for you or not, please watch this example of Richard Flook using ACE with someone: https://youtu.be/magjTYTF3x0. To find a practitioner or learn more about the training, please go to: www.advancedclearingenergetics.com

ABOUT THE BOOK

This book has been written from a place of passion and compassion for helping those grieving. The immense pain of loss can be so debilitating and where to turn for help can be such a challenge. The aim of this book is to offer you a guiding hand through your own individual grieving experience. Step by step you will be offered some new perspectives on your feelings and thoughts and how your loss may be affecting you on physical, psychological, spiritual, and behavioural levels. Each chapter offers some practical tools and techniques to help you navigate your way through your grief, helping you from the rawness of loss to a place of peaceful integration – and beyond if you wish. This book offers a new and modern perspective of how to help yourself holistically.

ABOUT THE AUTHOR

Janice Thompson has combined her academic qualifications which include a master's degree in Psychology research with her practical experience of working as a therapist and trainer. For the past fifteen years she has dedicated herself to helping those who are grieving. She has developed and facilitates grief training for practitioners, regularly runs workshops on loss and grief, holds grief retreats and leads an online grief café where those grieving can come together and share experiences. Janice speaks on various aspects of grief at conferences and has participated in a wide variety of podcasts.

Janice's passion for working with those grieving began after finding some techniques and tools to help herself through the sudden loss of her husband at a young age. The realisation that her struggle to find peace was related to an earlier death in the family led her on a journey to understand grief and subsequently help others.

Janice enjoys a simple life in Shropshire, England, where she lives on her narrowboat with her partner and her dog, Dudley.

Printed in the United States
by Baker & Taylor Publisher Services